Between Silence and Strength

The Sculpture of Dietrich Klinge

Between Silence and Strength

The Sculpture of Dietrich Klinge

Joseph Antenucci Becherer

Frederik Meijer Gardens and Sculpture Park
Grand Rapids, Michigan

Museum Küppersmühle
Sammlung Grothe, Duisburg

Imprint

This catalogue has been published in conjunction with the exhibition Between Silence and Strength: The Sculpture of Dietrich Klinge organized by Frederik Meijer Gardens and Sculpture Park, Grand Rapids, Michigan and held at the Gardens from June 3 through September 5, 2005 and at the Museum Küppersmühle Sammlung Grothe, Duisburg from October 30 until November 27, 2005.

The exhibition is curated in Grand Rapids by Joseph Antenucci Becherer and in Duisburg by Hans Grothe.

First published in the United States of America in 2005 by Frederik Meijer Gardens and Sculpture Park 1000 East Beltline NE Grand Rapids, Michigan 49525 in part through the generosity of the Meijer Foundation and the Sculpture Society of Frederik Meijer Gardens and Sculpture Park.

ISBN: 0-9712034-6-6

Author: Joseph Antenucci Becherer

Translations from English:
Barbara Schäfer, Hattingen

Photography: Renate Deckers-Matzko, Heidelberg, (reliefs, p.53), Jo Efinger, Stuttgart, (model of Geoparin, p.22, 43), Dietrich Klinge, Weidelbach

Typeset: Jeannette Müller, Galerie von Braunbehrens, Munich

Color Separations:
Martin Frischauf, Schwabenrepro, Stuttgart

Printed and bound:
Fotolito Longo, Bozen

Trade distribution in Europe:
Freshup Publishing
Forststr. 86
70176 Stuttgart

Impressum

Der Katalog erscheint anlässlich der Ausstellung Between Silence and Strength: The sculpture of Dietrich Klinge, die vom 3. Juni bis 9. September 2005 von den Frederik Meijer Gardens, Grand Rapids, Michigan veranstaltet wird und anschließend vom Museum Kuppersmühle Sammlung Grothe in Duisburg gezeigt wird.

Die Ausstellung wird in Grand Rapids von Joseph Antenucci Becherer und in Duisburg von Hans Grothe kuratiert .

Erstausgabe in den Vereinigten Staaten von Amerika, 2005 von den Frederik Meijer Gardens and Sculpture Park.

ISBN: 3-938023-53-8

Autor: Joseph Antenucci Becherer

Übersetzung: Barbara Schäfer, Hattingen

Photographie:
Renate Deckers-Matzko, Heidelberg, (Reliefs, S.53), Jo Efinger, Stuttgart, (Geoparin, S.22, S.43), Dietrich Klinge, Weidelbach

Satz: Jeannette Müller, Galerie von Braunbehrens, München

Lithographie:
Martin Frischauf, Schwabenrepro, Stuttgart

Druck und Bindung:
Fotolito Longo, Bozen

Vertrieb in Europa:
Freshup Publishing
Forststr. 86
70176 Stuttgart

Contents
Inhalt

Vorbemerkung und Dank

In Zusammenarbeit mit dem Museum Küppersmühle gibt sich Frederik Meijer Gardens and Sculpture Park die Ehre, die richtungweisende Ausstellung „Between Silence and Strength: The Sculpture of Dietrich Klinge“ zu präsentieren. Diese Retrospektive in der Mitte seiner Karriere ist die erste umfassende Museumsausstellung des Künstlers in Deutschland und in den Vereinigten Staaten. Sie zeigt mehr als fünfunddreißig Bronzeplastiken und fünfundzwanzig grafische Werke, die der Künstler im Verlauf der letzten zwei Jahrzehnte geschaffen hat.
Von der Kunstkritik beachtet und viel gesammelt, gehört Dietrich Klinge zu den erstaunlichsten und ideenreichsten Künstlern heutiger Zeit. Seine Entscheidung, die Darstellung der menschlichen Figur in das Zentrum seiner Arbeit zu stellen, war wohl überlegt und beruht auf einer umfassenden Kenntnis alter und zeitgenössischer Meister und deren Werke. Die Weiterentwicklung stilistischer Merkmale basiert auf bewussten Entscheidungen und deren unmittelbarer Umsetzung, verbunden mit einer meisterlichen Beherrschung der Bearbeitung des Holzes und des Bronzegusses. Dies hat die Aufmerksamkeit öffentlicher und privater Sammler in Europa, Russland und jüngst auch in den Vereinigten Staaten erregt.
Die gegenwärtige Ausstellung wäre ohne die Anregungen und die Kenntnis von Hans Grothe und Gerhard Reinz nicht zu Stande gekommen. Ihr Wissen und ihre Unterstützung würdige ich in besonderer Weise. Weiterhin waren für die Erstellung dieses Projekts die Bemühungen von Albrecht Eichler, Inge Gayda, Norbert Dahlström und Walter Smerling unverzichtbar, Barbara Schäfer hat freundlicherweise den Text übersetzt, Linda Thompson hat dankenswerterweise Korrektur gelesen. Man kann den Mitarbeitern vom Museum Küppersmühle und Frederik Meijer Gardens and Sculpture Park zu ihren Bemühungen, eine außergewöhnliche Ausstellung möglich zu machen, gratulieren.
Fred und Lena Meijer in Grand Rapids in Verbindung mit dem Sculpture Advisory Committee zollen wir Anerkennung für ihre Entscheidung, die erste Skulptur Dietrich Klinges für eine öffentliche Sammlung zu erwerben und damit den Auslöser für die gegenwärtige Ausstellung zu geben. Erst seit Beginn diesen Jahres kann man Werke von Klinge an wichtigen Orten in New York, Chicago und St. Louis betrachten.
Zum Schluss gilt mein besonderer Dank dem Künstler. Die Bedeutung seines Werkes beruht auf der intensiven Wirkung auf die heutigen Betrachter und wird diese zweifellos für zukünftige Generationen aufgrund der starken Wirkung von Inhalt und Form behalten. Weiterhin gilt mein Dank Klinges Bereitschaft, über seine Arbeit mit mir bei zahlreichen Gelegenheiten in den letzten zwei Jahren zu sprechen. Dies waren erfreuliche und aufschlussreiche Gespräche.

Joseph Antenucci Becherer, Ph.D.
Director and Curator, Frederik Meijer Gardens & Sculpture Park
and Professor of Art History, Acquinas College

Forward and Acknowledgments

In collaboration with the Museum Küppersmühle, Frederik Meijer Gardens and Sculpture Park is honored to present the landmark exhibition, "Between Silence and Strength: The Sculpture of Dietrich Klinge." This mid-career retrospective is the artist's first large-scale, museum presentation in Germany and the United States. It features more than thirty-five bronzes and twenty graphic works the artist has executed over the course of the last two decades.

Critically acclaimed and eagerly collected, Dietrich Klinge is among the most prodigious and original sculptors working today. His decision to focus on the figure was duly deliberated and informed by a vast knowledge of historical and contemporary masters and monuments. Stylistic development has been measured, thoughtful and direct. This, combined with his mastery of carving and casting techniques, has captivated public and private collectors in Europe, Russia, and most recently the United States.

The present exhibition is indebted to the inspiration and foresight of Hans Groethe and Gerhard Reinz. Their wisdom and support is greatly appreciated. Further, the efforts of Albrecht Eichler, Inge Gayda, Norbert Dahlström and Walter Smerling have proved invaluable to the creation of this project. Bärbel Schäfer has generously translated the text and Linda Thompson has graciously served as the primary reader. The staff at both the Museum Küppersmühle and Frederik Meijer Gardens and Sculpture Park are to be congratulated for their efforts to create an outstanding installation.

In Grand Rapids, Fred and Lena Meijer, in conjunction with the Sculpture Advisory Committee are to be acknowledged for their vision in acquiring Dietrich Klinge's first sculpture to enter a public collection in the United States and encouraging the present exhibition. As recent as this year, Klinge's work has begun to appear in important venues in New York, Chicago, and St. Louis.

Finally, the most important acknowledgement goes to the artist. The significance of his work resonates strongly with audiences today and will undoubtedly nourish future generations due to the high caliber of thought and execution. Further, Klinge's willingness to discuss his work with me on numerous occasions over the course of the last two years has been a joyous, informative endeavor.

Joseph Antenucci Becherer, Ph.D.
Director and Curator, Frederik Meijer Gardens & Sculpture Park
and Professor of Art History, Aquinas College

8 **Grosser Trefree,**
Bronze, 2000, 4/6,
h. 56 1/2 inches
Höhe 143,5 cm

Gift of Fred and Lena Meijer

Between Silence and Strength

The Sculpture of Dietrich Klinge

By Joseph Antenucci Becherer, Ph.D.

Like a glacier in the dawn light, **Grosser Trefree** rests before the viewer. The boldness of the form is majestic. Although life-size, it projects a much grander scale. A connection to earth and the horizon is clear, and the challenge to the surrounding open spaces is forthright. Seated with arms locked, power is bound. However, the imagination measures the potential force of action. A commanding, crystalline quiet underscores the restraint. Bronze offers this sculpture the promise of physical endurance, but the psychological attraction for the audience exists between notions of quiet and power. **Grosser Trefree** factors significantly in the evolution of Dietrich Klinge's oeuvre. Specific to the present investigation, a retrospective survey, it represents both the culmination of nearly twenty years of steady experimentation with the human form and serves as a transitional talisman in the most current investigations of form and meaning. Klinge is among the most prodigious and original sculptors on the contemporary scene. His pensive figures initially carved in wood then painstakingly translated into bronze, are compelling and unique. Widely known and respected in his native Germany, his reputation attracts critical attention throughout Europe and Russia, and most recently, the United States.

*Schroff, abwehrend, kalt wie ein Gletscher, auf den die ersten Lichtstrahlen der Morgendämmerung fallen, verweilt die Figur „**Großer Trefree**“ vor dem Betrachter. Die erhabene Form lässt sie in ihrer Wirkung übermenschlich groß erscheinen. Sitzend mit verschränkten Armen bleibt die Kraft im Inneren der Plastik. Die Verbindung zwischen Erde und Horizont ist klar erkennbar, einerseits zeigt sich ein Widerstreit zwischen ihrem sie umgebenden, offenen Raum und ihrem eigenen Raum, den sie durch ihre verschränkten Arme, die ihre innere Kraft symbolisieren, einschränkt. So entsteht der Eindruck eines inneren Konfliktes – in Aktion treten zu wollen oder in der Zurückhaltung, der Ruhe zu verharren. Die Bronze unterstreicht den Zwiespalt zwischen Schweigen und Tun. „**Großer Trefree**“ nimmt eine Schlüsselrolle in der Entwicklung von Dietrich Klinges Gesamtwerk ein.*

In der vorliegenden retrospektiven Übersicht stellt diese Arbeit sowohl den Höhepunkt eines fast zwanzig Jahre dauernden, ständigen Prozesses des Experimentierens mit der menschlichen Figur dar, als auch einen Meilenstein in Bezug auf die neuere Entwicklung von Form und Ausdruck. Klinge gehört zu den erstaunlichsten und originellsten Bildhauern der zeitgenössischen Kunstszene. Seine nachdenklichen, zunächst in Holz ge-

10 **Model for a Big Sculpture III**
Entwurf für eine Große Figur III,
Bronze, 2004, 1/6,
h. 85 7/8 x 78 3/4 x 123 5/8 inches
218 x 200 x 314 cm

This exhibition is the premiere museum presentation in Germany and America. It traces the course of the sculptor's journey from the mid 1980s to the present and attempts to illuminate relevant biographical information. At the onset of his career, Klinge judiciously pondered his decision to engage with the human figure, the centerpiece of world art since prehistory, and its relevance to contemporary society. Therefore, his development can be understood as deliberate.

In a group of five sculptures initiated in 2003 and completed in 2004, Klinge created figures that vary appreciably from **Grosser Trefree**. Simultaneously writhing upward and rooting downward, **Model for a Big Sculpture III** is among the most dynamic. From the firmly grounded lower torso, this form pulsates with the rhythm of unfolding life. Legs and right arm aspire towards the earth but the serpentine neck, upper body and left arm yearn for the atmosphere above. The viewer bears witness to a measured, precious metamorphosis. The monumental scale of the figure and the physical contortions of its powerful elements differ from **Grosser Trefree**, but the bronze medium, tenants of style, and even a commanding sense of calm, remain. Taken together, these sculptures could mislead one to believe that the timeless battles of successive periods of artistic development that stretch back to Classicism versus Hellenism exist in near simultaneity within one artist. While postmodernism has ordained such a treatise for other artists, with Dietrich Klinge, stylistic development is thoroughly contemplated and, at times, cautiously incre-

schnitzten und dann sorgfältig in Bronze gegossenen Figuren sind unwiderstehlich und einzigartig.
In Deutschland als Künstler beachtet und etabliert gewinnen seine Arbeiten immer größere Aufmerksamkeit in der modernen europäischen Kunstszene sowie in Russland und den USA. Die Ausstellung ist seine erste Museumspräsentation in den USA. Sie verfolgt den Werdegang des Bildhauers seit Mitte der achtziger Jahre bis in die heutige Zeit und akzentuiert biografische Informationen , die für seine Entwicklung maßgeblich sind. Die Auseinandersetzung mit der menschlichen Figur, seit jeher Mittelpunkt der Weltkunst und auch ihre Relevanz für die heutige Gesellschaft ist zentrales Thema bei Klinge. Er nähert sich diesem Ziel, indem er akribisch die Vorbilder seit der Frühgeschichte studiert und ihre stilistischen Merkmale zu begreifen versucht. So basiert seine Entwicklung auf bewussten und wohl durchdachten Entscheidungen.

In einem Zyklus von fünf Skulpturen, im Jahre 2003 begonnen und 2004 abgeschlossen, schuf Klinge Figuren, die sich erheblich von ***„Großer Trefree"*** *unterscheiden. Zu den dynamischsten gehört die Arbeit* ***„Entwurf für eine große Skulptur III"****. Der Unterleib, der rechte Arm und das linke Bein ruhen ruhig auf der Erde, während der gewundene Hals, Oberkörper und der linke Arm eine sich entfaltende Lebensfreude zeigen, die sich im Lösen von der Erde und dem Hinwenden in den Raum manifestiert. Dies macht den Betrachter zum Zeugen einer behutsamen und bedeutungsvollen Metamorphose. Die monumentale Größe der Figur und die gedrehten Gliedmaße unterscheiden sie von* ***„Großer Trefree"****, aber Bronze, verschiedene Stilelemente*

mental. In fact, several critical intellectual and stylistic developments occur in the brief time span between the two aforementioned sculptures.

With a career marked by steadied and vital achievements in both form and meaning, Dietrich Klinge is an innovative and consequential figurative sculptor. Like Henry Moore or George Segal in the last century, the artist remains thoroughly engaged with a subject ignored or maligned by noteworthy contemporaries. To the novice eye, the gesture, demeanor and even texture of Klinge's sculpture advances general characteristics of early 20th century Expressionism or even later Neo-Expressionism. However, close examination of his work reveals a careful consideration of materials and a thoroughly contemplated execution of forms that penetrates well beyond any gestural or topical neurosis. Even the consideration of one of his many bronze heads, a symbolic condensation of the entire the human form, a reverence for the original wood and the assured characteristics of carving through which the image is initially fashioned delivers a touchstone that can address soulful issues of the human experience. Throughout his career, the premeditated qualities of the sculptor's style parallels the penetration of momentary individual or cultural anxieties. Timeless and universal themes contemplate the actions of want, desire, possibility and loss. Here is the essence and spirit of masters like Albrecht Dürer or Rembrandt that Klinge admired early in his childhood.

Dietrich Klinge was born in 1954 in Heilingenstadt, Germany six miles

und auch die beherrschende Stimmung der Ruhe ist beiden gemeinsam. Und doch unterscheiden sie sich elementar in ihrem Ausdruck. Betrachtet man die beiden Skulpturen, könnte man zu dem falschen Schluss gelangen, die immerwährenden Kämpfe der aufeinanderfolgenden Phasen der künstlerischen Entwicklung Klassik – Hellenismus existierten gleichzeitig in einem Künstler. Während in der Postmodernen bei anderen Künstlern solche Gleichzeitigkeiten geschehen, ist die stilistische Entwicklung bei Dietrich Klinge wohl durchdacht und im Laufe der Zeit vorsichtig erweitert. Tatsächlich finden aber innerhalb einer kurzen Zeitspanne der Entstehung der beiden o.a. Arbeiten mehrere entscheidende Entwicklungen statt.

In seinem Werk, das sich in Form und Inhalt stetig und vital weiterentwickelt, erweist sich Dietrich Klinge als innovativer und konsequenter Bildhauer. Wie im letzten Jahrhundert Henry Moore und George Segal konzentriert sich der Künstler auf ein Thema, das von anerkannten Zeitgenossen ignoriert oder verleumdet wird. Das ungeübte Auge könnte Gestik, Haltung und Oberfläche von Klinges Plastiken mit dem Expressionismus oder sogar dem späten Neoimpressionismus in Verbindung bringen. Eine nähere Auseinandersetzung mit seinem Werk zeugt jedoch von der sorgfältigen Überlegung bei der Auswahl des Materials und einer gründlich bedachten Ausführung der Form, die hinterfragt, was über neurotisches Gehabe und aktuellen Zeitgeist hinausgeht. Auch die Auseinandersetzung mit einem seiner vielen Bronzeköpfe, deren Form er in sicherer Bearbeitung aus Holz herausarbeitet, wirft die Fragen nach dem Sinn menschlichen Seins

within the eastern border of a then divided nation. To the larger cultural world, the town is most well known as the birthplace of the Renaissance sculptor Tilman Riemenschneider. Klinge's parents worked in the sales division of a shoe manufacturer. His only sibling, an older brother, was active and gregarious while he was quiet, introspective and frequently immobile. "My parents worried about me because I would sit and stare for long periods of time," the artist states, "my brother became very athletic, but I was not interested in such things as a youth." The extended family was Roman Catholic, with a notable number of priests creating an environment that the artist later described as "quite fundamentalist in a heavily Protestant region." Klinge's maternal grandmother lived in "the West", in the town of Fritzlar; his mother often crossed the border in order to visit family and return with goods and supplies. In 1958, the parents decided to emigrate. The father and boys traveled under the auspices of an authorized day trip and left the mother behind in order to dissuade suspicious border guards. Soon after, she crossed the border over vast farm fields to rejoin her family at her mother's home. In addition to enjoying the companionship of his grandmother during this period, Klinge was drawn to the ardent Romanesque figurative sculptures in the town's cathedral.

The family moved to Stuttgart in 1960 where Klinge's father worked in the offices of the Mercedes shoe factory and his mother found work with the postal service. They lived in apartment block housing where as many as twenty-five families with swarms

auf. Sein Werk zeigt eine Weiterentwicklung in der Form seiner Skulpturen und deren inhaltlicher Durchdringung individueller und gesellschaftlicher Lebensängste, zeitlose, alle Menschen betreffende Fragen nach Wünschen, Hoffnungen, Möglichkeiten und dem Verlust. Fragen, die Werke von Albrecht Dürer und Rembrandt aufwerfen, die Klinge seit seiner frühen Kindheit bewundert.

Dietrich Klinge wurde 1954 in Heiligenstadt geboren, sechs Kilometer östlich der Grenze, des damals geteilten Deutschlands. Der kulturell interessierteren Welt ist die Stadt bekannt als der Geburtsort des Renaissance- Bildhauers Tilman Riemenschneider. Klinges Eltern arbeiten im eigenen Schuhgeschäft. Sein älterer Bruder ist unternehmungslustig und gesellig, während er selbst ruhig und introvertiert ist. „Meine Eltern machten sich Sorgen um mich, weil ich nur dasaß und über einen langen Zeitraum beobachtete. Mein Bruder war sehr sportlich, aber solche Dinge haben mich in meiner Jugend nicht interessiert." Die Familie ist katholisch, mehrere Familienmitglieder wurden Priester, wodurch eine Situation entsteht, die der Künstler später als „fundamentalistisch in einer erzprotestantischen Region" bezeichnet. Klinges Großmutter mütterlicherseits lebt im „Westen" in Fritzlar. Die Mutter fährt oft über die Grenze, um ihre Familie zu besuchen und kehrt mit Lebensmitteln und für das tägliche Leben notwendigen Dingen zurück. Im Jahre 1958 beschließen die Eltern in den Westen zu fliehen. Der Vater und die Jungen reisen mit einem Tagesvisum aus. Die Mutter bleibt zunächst zurück, um nicht das Misstrauen der Grenzbeamten zu wecken. Kurze Zeit später folgt sie der Familie auf

of children might reside in one block. Within this commotion, the hushed and pensive six-year-old began an odyssey in visual arts. Klinge recalls, "at this time I began to draw all the time and the very best present I can remember from my childhood was a drawing book." He was also fascinated with a framed reproduction of Dürer's renowned **Praying Hands**, which hung in his parents' bedroom. "I went to the library next to the school and asked for books on this artist and then began to copy his engravings and etchings." He continues, "From here I also began to study books on Rembrandt." In keeping with the reproduction of prints that captivated him, Klinge drew primarily in black and white, and while other children drew large, gestural images, he preferred to make small drawings. At fourteen, he began to experiment with printmaking, carving, and even enamel work after school at the local youth house. He acquired copper plates and began to work in drypoint at home. Astonishingly, he even made his own press from the discarded ringer of a washing machine. Such ingenuity would become hallmark of his mature career.

Although the linear clarity of those historical images he copied remains indelible for Klinge, the imagery served equally as a witness to the timeless drama of the human condition he would soon explore directly. At eighteen, he witnessed the extreme difficulties and suffering of life during an extended stay in Nepal and India (including Sikkim). From outside his own culture, his ideas about life and death, imagination and reality were challenged and, in turn, ex-

Umwegen. Die Familie trifft sich im Hause der Großmutter in Fritzlar wieder. Klinge genießt die Zeit, in der die Familie bei der Großmutter lebt. Die romanischen Figuren am Dom zu Fritzlar hinterlassen bei ihm einen bleibenden Eindruck. Im Jahre 1960 zieht die Familie nach Stuttgart, wo Klinges Vater im Büro der Schuhfabrik Mercedes arbeitet. Seine Mutter findet eine Stelle bei der Post. Sie leben in einem Wohnblock, zusammen mit 25 kinderreichen Familien. In dieser unruhigen Atmosphäre beginnt der stille und nachdenkliche Sechsjährige seine Odyssee in die bildende Kunst. Klinge erinnert sich: „In dieser Zeit begann ich unentwegt zu zeichnen und das schönste Geschenk meiner Kindheit, an das ich mich erinnern kann, war ein Zeichenbuch." Er ist fasziniert von einer gerahmten Reproduktion von Dürers ***„Betende Hände"****, die im Schlafzimmer seiner Eltern hängt. „Ich ging in die Bücherei neben der Schule und lieh mir Bücher über diesen Künstler aus und begann, seine Kupferstiche und Holzschnitte zu kopieren und Bücher über Rembrandt zu lesen. Die Reproduktion der Bilder, die ihn faszinieren, zeichnet Klinge hauptsächlich in Schwarz-Weiß, im Gegensatz zu den Bildern anderer Kinder sind Klinges Bilder kleinformatig. Mit vierzehn beginnt er nach der Schule im Jugendhaus Drucke herzustellen, Holz zu bearbeiten und mit Emaille zu experimentieren. Er beschafft sich Kupferplatten und beginnt zu Hause mit der Kaltnadel zu arbeiten. Aus einer alten Wäschemangel baut er seine erste Druckerpresse. Dieser Erfindungsreichtum bleibt Kennzeichen seines späteren Werks.*

Nicht nur die klare Linienführung der historischen Bilder, die er kopiert, blei-

panded. When he returned to Germany, he worked in a junkyard and prepared himself for the entrance examination to Stuttgart's highly regarded art academy, Staatlichen Akademie der Bildenden Kunst. Admitted in June of 1973, he began formal study in the following October. Klinge soon discovered an environment much different than he had imagined; most of the students came from upper middle class backgrounds and only a few had seen larger aspects of the world. His experiences in Asia and current work in the junkyard set him apart. Undeterred, he concentrated on the foundation curriculum and resumed creating etchings. Peter Grau was his first drawing professor while Gunther Bohmer and his successor, Rudolf Schoofs, taught graphic illustration. In 1979, Klinge created his first stone sculpture and for a period executed one work every month. Although he completed the course of study for drawing and graphic work in 1980, he formally embarked on the sculpture program working under Herbert Baumann and Alfred Hirdlicka later the same year. He completed the program in 1984.

Klinge spent more than a decade at the Academy supporting himself through odd jobs and manual labor. In discussing this period, he describes how thoroughly he made use of the facilities and equipment the institution offered. Yet, for his voracious appetite for experimentation and discovery, he did not exhibit his work until 1989. He admits, "I made a decision to work completely for myself during this period" – a personal declaration of this time as one of technical and stylistic incubation. Although a lengthy discussion is beyond the

ben unauslöschlich in seiner Erinnerung, sie dienen ihm auch als Zeugen des unendlichen Dramas menschlichen Lebens, das er bald aus erster Hand erfahren sollte. Mit achtzehn wird er während eines längeren Aufenthalts in Indien, Nepal und Sikkim Zeuge der extrem schwierigen Lebensbedingungen und des menschlichen Leids in diesen Ländern. Diese Erfahrungen außerhalb seiner eigenen Kultur stellen für seine Vorstellungen von Leben und Tod, Imagination und Realität eine Herausforderung und gleichzeitig eine geistige Erweiterung dar. Als er nach Deutschland zurückkehrt, arbeitet er auf einem Schrottplatz und bereitet sich auf die Aufnahmeprüfung für Stuttgarts angesehener Kunstakademie der „Staatlichen Akademie der Bildenden Künste" vor. Im Juni 1973 wird er an der Akademie angenommen und beginnt im Oktober 1973 sein Studium. Bald entdeckt Klinge, dass das universitäre Umfeld völlig anders ist, als er es sich vorgestellt hatte. Die meisten Studenten stammen aus der oberen Mittelschicht und nur wenige haben eine Vorstellung von den größeren Zusammenhängen in der Welt. Seine Erfahrungen in Asien und bei seiner Arbeit auf dem Schrottplatz grenzen ihn von den anderen ab. Davon unberührt, konzentriert er sich auf sein Grundstudium und beginnt wieder Radierungen zu schaffen. Peter Grau ist sein erster Zeichenlehrer. Günter Böhmer und sein Nachfolger, Rudolf Schoofs, lehren ihn freie Grafik. Im Jahre 1979 schafft Klinge seine erste Steinskulptur und eine Zeit lang gestaltet er eine Arbeit pro Monat. Obwohl er das Studium für Zeichnung und Grafik im Jahre 1980 abschließt, schreibt sich Klinge noch im selben Jahr für den Studiengang „Bildhauerei" unter der Leitung von Herbert

Trylogy, oe.can.
Trilogie, oe.can.

series of 183 etchings in 8 chapters, 1982 - 1985, edition of 15
Zyklus von 183 Radierungen in 8 Kapiteln, 1982 - 1985, Auflage: 15 Exemplare
chapter 6, 1984, leaf 2, h. 13 x 15 3/4, h.12 15/16 x 6 2/3 inches
Kapitel 6, 1984, Blatt 2, 33 x 40 cm, 32,9 x 17 cm

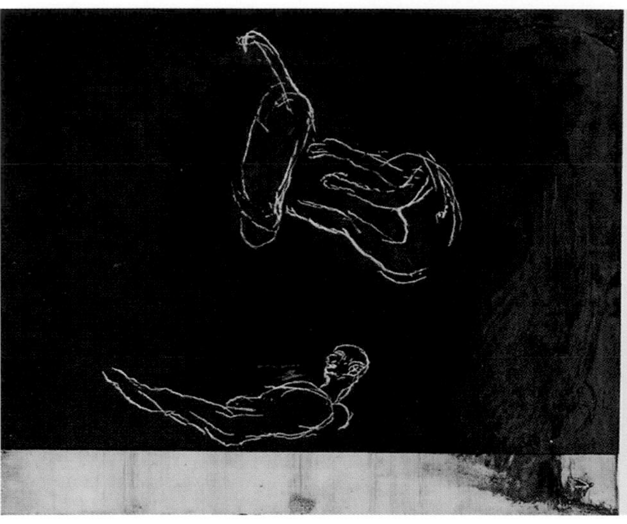

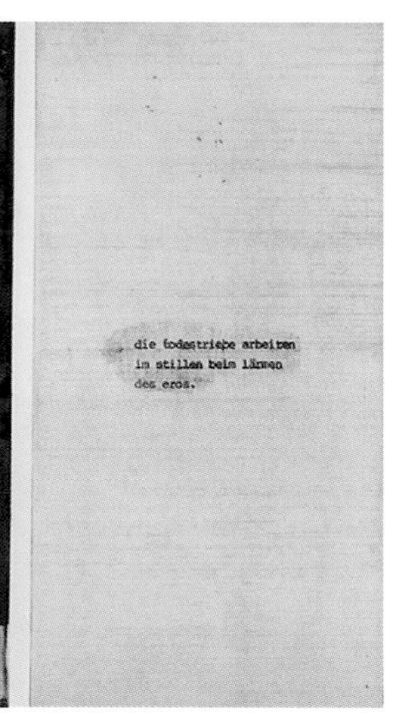

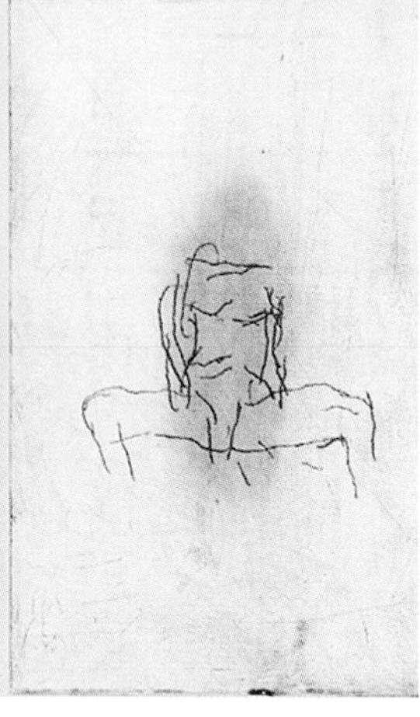

Trylogy, oe.can.
Trilogie, oe.can.

series of 183 etchings in 8 chapters, 1982 - 1985, edition of 15
Zyklus von 183 Radierungen in 8 Kapiteln, 1982 - 1985, Auflage: 15 Exemplare
chapter 7, 1984, leaf 14, h. 13 x 15 3/4, h. 12 5/16 x 7 2/3 inches
Kapitel 7, 1984, Blatt 14,
33 x 40 cm, 32,7 x 19,5 cm

scope of the present survey, notice must be made of an expansive graphic project that occupied the artist's attention during the mid 1980s. **Trilogy**, 1982-1985, is an epic series of 183 etchings arranged in eight chapters. The complex narrative and personal iconography is best described in the artist's own words as "an attempt to understand the world at this time." However, numerous characteristics of the work at large illuminate qualities that inform innovative developments in Klinge's oeuvre in the ensuing decades. The bold use of line and contour, honest suggestion of texture, and the cautious relationship between the imagery and the nature of

Baumann und Alfred Hrdlicka ein. Dieses Studium schließt er im Jahre 1984 ab.

Klinge studiert mehr als ein Jahrzehnt an der Akademie und verdient sich in dieser Zeit seinen Lebensunterhalt mit Gelegenheitsjobs und harter körperlicher Arbeit. Wenn man sich mit ihm über diese Zeit unterhält, betont er, dass er alle sich ihm bietenden Ausstattungen der Akademie intensiv genutzt hat. Trotz seiner großen Experimentierfreude im künstlerischen Bereich und der Entdeckung neuer Ausdrucksmöglichkeiten hat er sein Werk erst 1989 ausgestellt. „Während dieser Zeit habe ich die Entscheidung getroffen, ausschließlich für mich selbst zu arbeiten.“ Eine persönliche Entscheidung, um sich technisch und stilistisch weiterentwickeln zu können. In der Mitte der 80iger entstand ein umfassendes grafisches Werk ***„Trilogie ÖK“****, 1982-1985. Es ist ein epischer Zyklus von 183 Radierungen aufgeteilt in acht Kapitel. Die komplexe, narrative und persönliche Ikonographie lässt sich am besten mit den eigenen Worten des Künstlers, „ein Versuch die Welt zu verstehen“, beschreiben. Zahlreiche Merkmale dieses Werkes weisen auf die innovative Entwicklung der nächsten zehn Jahre im Oeuvre Klinges hin. Die klare Linienführung und Kontur, Verknüpfung von Form und Inhalt in den Darstellungen, die einfühlsame Verbindung zwischen Bildsymbolik und verwendetem Material ist überzeugend. In besonderer Weise ist das wachsende Bewusstsein für die Ausdruckskraft des menschlichen Bildes hervorzuheben. Menschen werden in ihrer Isolation und Eindimensionalität, Unfähigkeit ihren Zustand zu verändern, dargestellt. Aber die Kraft der sie begrenzenden Linien und ihre Stel-*

materials is striking. Paramount is a growing awareness of the power of the human form. Here, it frequently depicts isolation and immobility, but the force of the descriptive outlines and position on the respective sheets renders them as a source of concentrated energy and emotion.

In 1986, Klinge initiated an uninterrupted commitment to the human form with a series of heads. **Head of Holofernes**, 1987, is a poignant early example. The work is marked by rough textures and specific surface lacerations that speak to the carving process. Originally executed in wood, the sculpture was then cast in bronze.

lung im Bild, lassen sie zu einer Quelle geballter Energie und großer Emotionen werden.

1986 schafft Klinge eine Reihe von Köpfen, die seine Arbeit beherrschende, kontinuierliche Auseinandersetzung mit der menschlichen Gestalt dokumentiert. Der ***„Kopf des Holofernes“****, 1987, ist hierfür ein frühes eindringliches Beispiel. Die Arbeit zeichnet sich durch seine zerklüftete und die beim Vorgang des Bearbeitens bewusst gemachten tiefen Einschnitte in die Oberfläche aus. Ursprünglich wird das Modell in Holz gearbeitet. Die eigentliche Skulptur ist die gegossene Bronze. Diese originelle Methode der Realisierung*

Head of Holofernes
Kopf Holofernes
Bronze, 1987, 0/8
h. 7 inches
Höhe 18 cm

◂◂

Head Crucifix
Kopf Kruzifix
Bronze, 1988, 0/8
h. 6 inches
Höhe 15 cm

From this point forward, this unique method of realizing a work is fundamental to the artist's repertoire and witness to both his mastery of the carving and casting processes. In both **Head of Holofernes** and **Head Crucifix**, 1988, the great sense of mass suggests the density of stone and perhaps the sculptures are informed by vestiges of the noted series of stone carvings the artist executed from 1979 through the mid 1980s. But the anonymous, physical reality of each work vies for attention against

einer Plastik zeugt von der besonderen Beherrschung der Formgebung des Holzmodells und dessen Transformation in Bronze. Bei beiden Köpfen ***„Holofernes“*** *und* ***„Kruzifix“****, 1988, suggeriert das Gefühl von großer Masse dem Betrachter, sie seien aus Stein. Vielleicht verweisen sie auf die o.a. Serie von Steinplastiken, die der Künstler von 1979 bis in die Mitte der achtziger Jahre schuf. Die anonyme, körperliche Präsenz jeder einzelnen Arbeit bildet ein Spannungsfeld zu ihrer emotionalen und psychischen Kraft. Die*

its emotional and psychological power. The energy of an entire figure is held captive in a single object, an invented relic. Although the works read as skulls, the reflections upon or desires for the actions and passions of a life lived are discernable. Intellectually charged and physically startling, either sculpture seems perfectly suited for a contemporary library of St.

Energie der gesamten Figur scheint in diesen Köpfen gefangen zu sein. Obwohl beide Köpfe Schädel sind, werden in ihnen ihre Gedanken, Verlangen nach Taten und die Leiden ihres gelebten Lebens transparent. Geistig wach, jedoch körperlich verfallen scheinen beide Köpfe prädestiniert für die zeitgenössische Bibliothek St. Hieronimus (in der Zelle). Spätere Bei-

Head no. 103
Kopf Nr. 103
Bronze, 1997, 0/9
h. 7 inches
Höhe 18 cm

Head no. 107 ►►
Kopf Nr. 107
Bronze, 1997, 0/9
h. 7 5/8 inches
Höhe 19,5 cm

Jerome. Later examples of this genre are more implicit as heads than crania. Two from 1997, **Head Number 103** and **Head Number 107**, are equally stoic and elegant. Rather than contemplative artifacts, each possesses a wary authority that proposes the presence of an individual. Stylized facial features are pronounced with intentionally uneven contours. They are more individualistic and humane than the cycladic ancestors of figurative sculpture's early history. The surface of each intentionally but subtly betrays carving techniques and the nature of the original wood is therefore more keenly understood. Although intrinsically and extrinsically potent, head or skull imagery is but part of Dietrich Klinge's development.

*spiele dieser Reihe sind eher als Köpfe denn als Schädel erkennbar. Die **Köpfe „Nr. 103 und Nr. 107"** sind gleichermaßen stoisch und elegant. Mehr als kontemplative Schöpfungen, besitzt jeder eine eigene Autorität, die ihn als Individuum präsent macht. Stilisierte Gesichtszüge werden bewusst durch unebene Konturen dargestellt. Sie sind individualistischer und menschlicher als die cykladischen Vorbilder aus der Frühgeschichte figürlicher Plastiken. Die Oberfläche eines jeden Kopfes verrät auf subtile Weise den Bearbeitungsprozess des Holzes und die Struktur des verarbeiteten Holzes. Obwohl intrinsisch und extrinsisch ausdrucksstark, ist die Darstellung von Köpfen oder Schädeln nur ein Teil von Dietrich Klinges künstlerischer Entwicklung.*

In the decade between these sets of heads, Klinge's repertoire expanded guardedly. Beyond the iconic heads, references to the whole of the human form are noteworthy. **The Fall**, 1993, is composed of a large cage-like structure against which a long, four-pronged bar precariously rests. At the base of the bars lies a head. The work bears witness to a series of installations Klinge produced in the late 1980s and early 1990s wherein disparate elements, often in different materials, are placed in relation to one and other. The subject matter is frequently a melding of the artist's personal vision with that of mythic legends, but the narrative compositions are ultimately an experiment with the figure. All of the elements were created by the artist even though there is the suggestion of found objects. Duchampian at base, the combination implies the presence of a human form and distills an action of the recent past. **Autokatalyse VI**, 1992, is a slightly earlier work, which compresses action and emotion further inward. The large bronze is composed of a head attached atop an elongated box. Two tapered poles are fixed to the top portion of the box on either side of the head. Although the artist fashions the mask-like head and poles, the box was made from old wood; all was then cast in bronze. **Autokatalyse VI** is unlike **The Fall** in that it is a single object and through the large block, indisputably conveys the trunk of a figure. Klinge divulges a struggle to convey the human form without creating a traditional figure. The mass of the sculpture may suggest force and the poles may intimate movement, but the form is paralyzed. As Klinge says, "the cube has power but (it) cannot do anything." Viewers

In den zehn Jahren, die zwischen dem Schaffen der o.a. Köpfe liegen, erweitert Klinge seinen Schaffensbereich. Die Entwicklung zu ersten Ganzkörperplastiken fällt in diesen Zeitraum. In ***„Der Fall“*** *1993 lehnt eine lange, viersprossige Stange unsicher an einem großen, käfigartigen Gebilde. Am unteren Ende der Stange ist ein Kopf. Die Arbeit ist ein Beispiel für eine Rei-*

The Fall
Der Fall
Bronze, 1993, 2/3
h. 94 inches
Höhe 240 cm

are first presented with a figure that cannot be and then asked to recognize the struggle between a desire to move and the ability to move; for now physical ambition remains cerebral.

With the totemic work **The Scream**, 1993, Klinge furthers his investigation of the figure and pursues the tensions of mass versus immobility. The sculpture is comprised of a successive series of roughly hewn blocks surmounted by a carved head. Each stepped block is outsized and intentionally references the human anatomy: upper torso, lower torso, and feet. Unlike the body utilized in **Autokatalyse VI**, the artist carves each block. Body and head are united as much by placement as by surface texture. Combined, the frontality of the work calls to mind classic examples of Egyptian sculpture whose rigid solidity betrays the secrets of preserva-

Autokatalyse VI
Bronze, 1992, 1/6
h. 30 3/4 x 46 7/8 x 18 1/2 inches
78 x 119 x 47cm

*he von Installationen, die Klinge in den späten achtziger und frühen neunziger Jahren schafft, in denen gegensätzliche Elemente, häufig aus unterschiedlichen Materialien in Beziehung gesetzt werden. Das Thema ist oft eine Symbiose aus persönlichen Visionen des Künstlers und Legenden, die der Mythologie entlehnt sind, aber die erzählerischen Kompositionen sind letztlich Experimente mit der menschlichen Figur. Eine etwas frühere Arbeit **„Autokatalyse VI“**, 1992, verlagert und komprimiert Handlung und Emotion mehr ins Innere. Die große Bronze besteht aus einer länglichen Kiste, auf deren Vorderseite ein Kopf angebracht ist. Zwei sich verjüngende Stangen sind an dem oberen Teil des Kastens auf beiden Seiten des Kopfes angebracht. **„Autokatalyse VI“** unterscheidet sich vom „Fall“ dadurch, dass sie nur aus einem Teil besteht und die Kiste unbestreitbar an einen menschlichen Torso erinnert, ohne den menschlichen Körper realitätsgetreu darzustellen. Klinge suggeriert die menschliche Gestalt, ohne sie in traditioneller Weise darzustellen. Die Masse der Skulptur **„Der Fall“** mag Kraft vermitteln und die Pfosten, Symbole für Arme, Bewegung andeuten, aber die Form ist paralysiert. Wie Klinge über die **„Autokatalyse VI“** sagt: „Der Kubus hat Kraft, aber er kann nichts tun“. Der Betrachter wird mit einer Figur konfrontiert, die so nicht sein kann und erkennt dann den Kampf zwischen dem Verlangen, sich zu bewegen und der Fähigkeit sich zu bewegen. Das körperliche Verlangen bleibt eine Sache des Kopfes.*

*Mit dem totemartige Werk **„Der Schrei“**, 1993, entwickelt Klinge seine Darstellung der menschlichen Figur weiter und verfolgt das Spannungs-*

tion and timelessness. In contrast to the generalized form of the blocks described in **The Scream**, the details of the facial features are clear. Ideas, wants, even the fervor of the subject are imagined, but its body is unable to act upon them. Stylistically, the sculpture is part of a small group of similar works over which Klinge uniformly states, "the sculptures exude strong feelings, but again they can do nothing." Further, he underscores the concept that these beings are not frozen, but bound. Thus realized, the inaudible anguish of the title begins to penetrate the psyche of the viewer: a powerful cry is trapped within.

feld zwischen Körperlichkeit und Unbeweglichkeit. Die Skulptur besteht aus aufeinandergesetzten, unregelmäßig behauenen Blöcken, auf denen ein geschnitzter Kopf ruht. Jeder treppenartige Block ist übergroß und ihre Anordnung folgt der menschlichen Anatomie: Oberkörper, Unterkörper und Füße. Anders als beim Körper in ***„Autokatalyse VI"*** *bearbeitet der Künstler jeden Block. Körper und Kopf bilden eher in ihrer Anordnung als ihrer Oberflächengestaltung eine Einheit. Die Frontalität des Werkes erinnert an klassische Beispiele ägyptischer Skulpturen, deren strenge Haltung die Geheimnisse der Bewahrung des Menschlichen und der Zeitlosigkeit verinnerlicht zu haben scheint. Im Gegensatz zu der einheitlichen Bearbeitung der Blöcke bei der Plastik* ***„Der Schrei"*** *sind die Details der Gesichtszüge deutlich herausgearbeitet. Stilistisch gehört die Skulptur zu einer kleinen Gruppe ähnlicher Arbeiten, über die Klinge feststellt: „Diese Skulpturen strahlen starke Emotionen aus, aber wieder können sie nichts tun." Weiter führt er aus, dass diese Geschöpfe nicht gefroren, sondern erstarrt sind. Wenn man das erkannt hat, beginnt die unhörbare Qual des Titels die Psyche des Betrachters zu druchdringen. Ein qualvoller Schrei ist in der Figur gefangen.*

Den Wendepunkt, sich von den strengen, geometrischen Formen zu lösen, zeigt die Bronzebüste ***„Geoparin"*** *1993. Die erstarrte Form der zuvor besprochenen Arbeiten wird durch die leichte Neigung des Kopfes auf einem säulenartigen Hals und die Asymmetrie der großen Brüste aufgelöst. Im Gegensatz zu den früheren Plastiken sind die Geschlechtsmerkmale bei dieser Figur klar erkennbar, gemäß Klin-*

The Scream
Der Schrei
Bronze, 1993, 0/6
h. 61 x 22 7/8 x 30 3/8 inches
155 x 58 x 77cm

Model of Geoparin
Skizze Geoparin
Bronze, 1993, unique
h. 2 inches
Höhe 4,9 cm

22 **Geoparin**
Bronze, 1993, 0/9
h. 26 3/4 inches
Höhe 68 cm

Geometry and rigidity begin to dissolve in a commanding bust sculpture. **Geoparin** is a pivotal bronze also of 1993. A rounded head is distanced from the imposing breasts by a columnar neck. The stiffness of the previously discussed sculptures releases with the slightest tilt of the head and the uneven description of the breasts. Sexless identity is replaced by an undeniable sexuality befitting Klinge's definition of "the female form of the world." It is the organic quality of the contours that ex-

*ges Definition von „der weiblichen Form der Welt". Sie strahlt eine größere Sinnlichkeit aus als die früheren Arbeiten. „**Geoparin**" wurde zuerst als winziges Modell konzipiert. Seit 1987 bis heute experimentiert er mit diesen kleinen Modellen – er nennt sie „die Kleinen" – , die weniger Modell, eher dreidimensionale Skizzen sind. Ursprünglich aus Wachs geformt, später in Bronze gegossen, dienen sie als Basis für formale Fragestellungen des Künstlers, die er auf die großen, geschnitzten Holzmodelle überträgt, um*

udes a greater sensuality than previously available. **Geoparin** was first realized as a tiny, palm size model. Less a maquette and more a three-dimensional sketch, Klinge began experimenting with these diminutive figures (anecdotally referred to as "the littles") in 1987 and will continue the practice through 2002. Initially created in wax and then cast in bronze, they function as objects of deliberation for the formal issues the artist wished to expand upon in large carvings, which in turn, are translated into bronze. **Geoparin** is the first in a long series of busts executed by the artist. In 1995, Klinge created a noteworthy example in **FoU**. An elongated bust, the bearing and frontality of the form recall **The Scream**. Yet the opposing asymmetry of facial features, shoulders and breasts, imbues the work with an aching restlessness that suggests the body's modest efforts to respond to the wishes of the mind. This suggestion of energy yearned for matches the mastery of carved surfaces and precise conversion into bronze. The integrity of the original wood and the studied, but expressive marks of the sculptor's subtractions, combine in a unique language in the final metal form. Here, Klinge gives evidence of technical virtuosity and a respectful sensitivity to materials at a moment when he has just embarked upon on his odyssey with the human figure.

Through a group of relief sculptures from the mid 1990s, the artist first explored descriptions of the human anatomy in its entirety. Although the format and aesthetic is markedly different than the previously discussed examples, Klinge reminds the viewer "that as with life, art does not always

*diese wiederum in Bronze zu gießen. **„Geoparin"** ist die erste einer großen Anzahl von Büsten. Ein erwähnenswertes Beispiel ist **„FoU"**, 1995, eine gestreckte Figur, die in Form und Frontalität an **„Der Schrei"** erinnert. Die konkurrierende Asymmetrie der Gesichtszüge, Schultern und Brüste, die eine als schmerzhaft empfundene Rastlosigkeit zeigt, steht im Gegensatz zur Unfähigkeit auf innerste Wünsche zu reagieren. Der Wunsch diese Energie freizusetzen, wird durch die meisterliche Bearbeitung der Holzoberfläche und deren Transformation in Bronze realisiert. Die Bronzeskulptur ist eindeutig, sie spricht eine Sprache, sie integriert die Elemente des Holzmodells und den expressiven, bildhauerischen Schaffensprozess und wird zu deren Symbiose. Die Plastik gibt Zeugnis von Klinges großer, handwerklicher Virtuosität und einem einfühlsamen Umgang mit den Werkstoffen genau zu dem Zeitpunkt, als er sich aufmacht, die menschliche Figur zu entdecken.*

In der Mitte der 90iger Jahre schafft der Künstler seine ersten Ganzkörperdarstellungen in mehreren gegossenen Reliefskulpturen. Obwohl Größe und ästhetischer Ausdruck sich wesentlich von den vorher besprochenen Arbeiten unterscheiden, macht Klinge dem Betrachter klar: „Das ist wie im wirklichen Leben, Kunst folgt nicht immer einer geraden Linie."
*Kleine Bronzereliefs spielen bereits in den früheren Installationen aus den späten 80igern und frühen 90igern eine Rolle, aber keine dieser Arbeiten besitzt die Ausmaße und Monumentälität des Reliefs **„Das Rad"** von 1994. Eine stürmisch sich bewegende Figur stürzt nach links. Rechts unten im Relief befinden sich zwei Reifen. Die Be-*

FoU (sawCH)
Bronze, 1995, 0/6
h. 39 inches
Höhe 99 cm

follow a straight line." Small bronze relief plates factor in several of the artist's earlier installations from the late 1980s and early 1990s, but none possess the measurable and tactile monumentality of **The Wheel** executed in 1994. A frenetically posed figure appears lunging from the left towards two circular forms at bottom right. Action is strikingly audacious but frozen as a prehistoric life captured in a piece of amber or sedimentary stone. As a child, Klinge collected fossils and studied the impressions of

wegung ist erstaunlich dynamisch, aber die Figur wirkt wie ein prähistorisches Insekt in einem Stück Bernstein eingeschlossen oder in eine Versteinerung gepresst. Als Kind sammelt Klinge Fossilien und beschäftigt sich intensiv mit Versteinerungen. Er konstatiert: „Zu dieser Zeit hatte ich Hemmungen traditionelle Ganzkörperskulpturen zu machen, aber die Reliefs sind wie Fossilien, in denen die Figur bereits gestorben ist."
Stille ist dem Künstler vertraut, aber weit zurückliegendes Leben wirkt be-

The Wheel
Das Rad
Bronze relief, 1994, unique
h. 81 7/8 x 100 inches
208 x 254 cm

petrified beings. Now he acknowledges, "I was afraid of making traditional full-figure sculptures at this time, but the reliefs are like fossils where the figure has already died." Stillness rings familiar for the artist, but a distant life is liberating, providing the opportunity to address the body beyond the self-imposed limitations of head and torso. Two reliefs of 1997, **Relief 20-04-11** and **Relief E-1**, are equally epic in scale, but present female bodies in more restrained poses. The former explores the figure in an arrested posture of self-inspection, but the latter is realized in a direct, almost didactic manner. Each figure possesses the studied but honest, sexual identity reminiscent of fertility figures from pre-history. The basic images purport a raw power that later inspires a series of prints, but the true vigor of these works as objects exists because of Klinge's pursuits regarding texture and patina. Each form is built up of coarse, at times jagged, surfaces against the moderately uneven, flinty background. Brooding earth tones ultimately unite each relief in the patina created and applied by the artist. Through these invented fossils, Klinge transitions into a breakthrough period of steadfast exploration in the late 1990s.

Solafam, 1998, is a life-size work in the round that builds upon critical achievements of the recent past and forecasts imminent developments with the full figure. Again, the carved head plays a significant role. Less geometrically pronounced, the base block and torso recall principle elements of **The Scream** while the arms are reminiscent of the appendages in **Autokatalyse VI**. Each of the ele-

freiend und bietet die Möglichkeit sich dem ganzen Körper, ohne die selbstauferlegte Beschränkung auf Torso und Kopf, zuzuwenden. Die Reliefs ***„Relief 20-04-11"*** *und* ***„Relief E-1"*** *sind in ihren Ausmaßen ähnlich. Sie stellen weibliche Figuren aber in zurückgenommener, beherrschter Haltung dar. Die Figur des ersten Reliefs scheint sich selbst in einer erstarrten Haltung zu beobachten, die zweite Figur ist frontal auf eine fast konstruierte Art dargestellt. Jede Figur stellt offen und selbstbewusst ihre Sexualität zur Schau, die an prähistorische Fruchtbarkeitsfiguren erinnert. Die grundlegenden Bildelemente des Reliefs mit ihrer geballten Kraft inspirieren Klinge später zu einem Grafikzyklus, aber die tatsächliche Energie dieser Werke als Objekte vermittelt sich durch die Bearbeitung der Oberfläche und deren Patina. Die Oberfläche einer jeden Figur ist zerklüftet, manchmal schartig und hebt sich dadurch vom leicht unebenen, steinartig wirkenden Hintergrund ab. Diese geschaffenen Fossilien kennzeichnen einen Durchbruch Klinges in seiner beständigen Auseinandersetzung mit der menschlichen Figur in den späten 90igern.*

„Solafam" *, 1998 ist eine lebensgroße von allen Seiten zu betrachtende Plastik, die aus den Entwicklungen der jüngsten Vergangenheit resultiert und die bevorstehende Weiterentwicklung der Vollplastik ankündigt. Auch hier spielt der geschnitzte Kopf eine entscheidende Rolle. Weniger geometrisch dargestellt, verweisen der Sockel und der Torso auf grundlegende Darstellungselemente der Plastik* ***„Der Schrei"****, während die Arme an die Gliedmaße in* ***„Autokatalyse VI"*** *erinnern. Jedes der Elemente scheint wie eine unabhängige, emphatische Ver-*

Relief 20 - 04 - 11
Bronze, 1997, 1/6
h. 54 1/3 x 41 1/3 inches
140 x 100 cm

Relief E - 1
Bronze, 1997, 3/6
h. 71 7/12 x 33 1/2 inches
180 x 86 cm

26 **Solafam**
Bronze, 1998, 0/6
h. 68 1/2 x 29 x 30 inches
174 x 74 x 77cm

ments reads as independent, emphatically denying the organic whole witnessed in the reliefs. “I was apprehensive of the whole figure, but used parts to create the whole,” Klinge says reflecting on the sculpture, “human beings are parts held together.” **Solafam** is therefore a type of assemblage, but the restraint and inner ten-

*leugnung der organischen Ganzheit, die den Reliefs zueigen war. „Ich hatte Bedenken eine Vollplastik zu schaffen, aber benutzte Teile, um das Ganze darzustellen“, sagt Klinge reflektierend über diese Plastik: „Menschen sind Teile, die zusammengehalten werden.“ **„Solafam“** ist deshalb ihrem Typ nach eine zusammengesetzte Fi-*

sions of earlier work begin to release. Firmly grounded by the large base, the slender vertical elements appear willowy; the simple, uneasy curves of neck and arms attempt bodily grace. According to the artist, the title proposes an exchange, "a give and take." For the first time, one of Klinge's sculptures strains towards the viewer as the power of a centered mass guardedly extends into the immediate space. The relationship between object in space as well as subject and audience has been modified even if the true physical and intellectual force of the figure remains within. Klinge admits to a direct sensuality with this work, but the overriding sense of self-possession is more striking to the audience. In dramatic contrast, a major work of the following year exudes an unprecedented, raw carnality the viewer cannot escape.

If an initial navigation of form in space occurs with **Solafam**, now a masterful voyage is experienced in **Nellie Angel**, 1999. The head tilts noticeably to the right and the facial features are distinctly off-centered. A long, sinuous neck simultaneously twists and leans forward. Shoulders are daringly uneven accentuating the commanding irregularities of the breasts. When logically compared with **Geoparin**, an earlier incarnation of the female bust, the divergence of forms is arresting. However, most notable is the absence of frontality so insistent in Klinge's earlier sculptures. **Nellie Angel** rewards visual experience from all sides. Masterfully, the interpretation of the form varies according to the position of inspection: a fertility deity from the front, a rebuking or conversely consoling companion from the respective

gur, bei der sich aber die beherrschten, inneren Spannungen, die früheren Werken innewohnte, zu lösen beginnen. Der große Sockel steht fest auf dem Boden, die schmalen, vertikalen Elemente erscheinen überschlank. Der Kontrast zwischen dem kubusartigen Körper und den gewölbten Armen und Nacken verleiht der Figur eine körperliche Anmut. Nach Ansicht des Künstlers beinhaltet der Titel einen Tausch, „ein Geben und Nehmen". Zum ersten Mal scheint sich eine von Klinges Skulpturen auf den Betrachter zuzubewegen , als ob die Masse der Plastik, die sie an einen Ort fixiert, sich in den sie unmittelbar umgebenden Raum ausbreitet. Das Verhältnis zwischen Objekt im Raum gleichwie Subjekt und Betrachter hat sich verändert, selbst wenn die physische und geistige Kraft der Figur noch immer nach innen gerichtet ist. Klinge gesteht eine unmittelbar sinnliche Betrachtung seiner Arbeit zu, aber der überschreitende Sinn der Selbstaneignung des Werkes ist für den Betrachter intensiver.
Im völligen Gegensatz zu der oben beschriebenen Plastik zeigt ein Hauptwerk des folgenden Jahres eine unverhohlene, offen dargestellte körperliche Sinnlichkeit, deren Wirkung der Betrachter sich nicht entziehen kann.

*Wenn **„Solafam"** eine erste Annäherung an das Spannungsfeld von Form und Raum auslöst, so stellt **„Nellie Angel"**, 1999, eine deutliche Weiterentwicklung auf diesem Weg dar. Der Kopf der Figur neigt sich deutlich nach rechts und die Gesichtszüge sind dezentriert. Der lange, gebogene Hals ist nach vorn gerichtet. Die Schultern sind unterschiedlich hoch und unterstreichen die unregelmäßigen Brüste. Vergleicht man diese Büste mit **„Geoparin"**, einer früheren Darstellung ei-*

Nellie Angel
Bronze, 1999, 0/6
h. 30 inches
Höhe 76 cm

sides, a mannered, corporeal mystery from the rear. Ultimately, the vivacity of this sculpture is achieved through the artist's handling of surfaces. The inherent nature of the wood combined with the gestural character of the carving, often executed with power tools, unites in the final bronze form. As a result, the sculpture conveys an emotive authority sympathetic with certain currents in the history of art. "People see power in the work which they associate with Expressionism, African art, or even with contemporary artists like Baselitz, but like Romanesque sculpture the power exists within the work," Klinge states. For him, the validity of interior life and hush of contemplation is potent and delivers the work from the confines of momentary personal or cultural trends towards greater universality. Neither simply Germanic nor Post-Modern by definition, the work has broader relevance beyond a specific moment in time.

Discussing the material qualities of the sculpture leads to the clarification that it is extremely rare for the sculptor to exhibit his efforts in wood. For Klinge the resulting form in metal is the work of art. He insists, "When I see the bronze, I no longer see the wood." However, the original material is integral in defining the final form and makes a strong connection between Klinge and traditions within the history of German art. "Wood is a cultural thing and it says something about the social rank of the artist," he shares, "but it is also difficult to get good stone." Such ideas connect Klinge to medieval and Renaissance epochs when bronze and marble reigned supreme as much as to 20th century trends when the use of wood

ner weiblichen Büste, erkennt man interessante Unterschiede. Der bemerkenswerteste ist das Fehlen der Frontalität, die in Klinges früheren Plastiken häufig zu finden war. ***„Nellie Angel"*** *kann von allen Seiten betrachtet werden. Meisterhaft, wie die Interpretation der Figur sich mit dem Blickwinkel zur Plastik verändert. Eine Fruchtbarkeitsgöttin von vorn, eine tadelnde, aber auch tröstende Gefährtin von der jeweiligen Seite, ein körperliches Mysterium von hinten. Letztlich wird die Lebendigkeit dieser Figur durch die Bearbeitung der Oberfläche durch den Künstler erreicht. Die Oberflächenstruktur des Holzes in seiner charakteristischen Bearbeitung, die häufig mit einer Kettensäge ausgeführt wird, geht mit der endgültigen Plastik in Bronze eine Symbiose ein. Das Ergebnis könnte sich in seiner emotionalen Ausstrahlung mit bestimmten Richtungen der Kunstgeschichte in Verbindung bringen lassen. „Die Menschen sehen die Kraft in meiner Arbeit, die sie mit dem Expressionismus, Afrikanischer Kunst oder sogar mit zeitgenössischen Künstlern wie Baselitz assoziieren, aber wie bei romanischen Skulpturen existiert die Kraft im Inneren der Arbeit", sagt Klinge. Für ihn ist das Innenleben und die Stille der Kontemplation wichtig. Das lässt seine Arbeit über die Grenzen momentaner, persönlicher und kultureller Trends hinauswachsen hin zu einer größeren Allgemeingültigkeit. Weder nur deutsch noch postmodern besitzt sein Werk eine weitergehende Bedeutung, die den Moment der Zeit überdauert.*

Setzt man sich mit dem Material Holz als Werkstoff für die Modelle auseinander, wird einem klar, dass Klinge nur sehr selten seine Werke in diesem

finally charged against tradition. He sensitively expands the discussion of wood to address the tree itself, "the wood has many stories: there is the growth of the tree over time, and the wood I use represents the lifetime of the tree, and then there is my work on the wood." When the carved wood original is conveyed in bronze, the artist grants the tree longevity unavailable to organic materials; how sympathetic this is to the manner in which the forces of nature and time combine to create fossils.

Nellie Angel is but one of the major accomplishments of 1999. As noted in the opening of the text, this is the critical moment when Dietrich Klinge first addresses the full figure. **Grosser Trefree** is one of seven figures created in 1999 and 2000. In truth, the

Material ausstellt. Für ihn ist nur die in Bronze gegossene Form das Kunstwerk. Er insistiert: „Wenn ich die Bronzeplastik sehe, sehe ich nicht mehr das Holzmodell." Das Holzmodell ist jedoch integraler Bestandteil der endgültigen Ausführung und zeigt eine enge Verbindung zwischen Klinge und den Traditionen der deutschen Kunstgeschichte auf. „Holz ist ein Kulturgut und sagt etwas über den gesellschaftlichen Status des Künstlers aus, denn es ist schwieriger und kostspieliger an qualitativ guten Stein heranzukommen", führt Klinge aus. In solchen Überlegungen stellt Klinge eine Verbindung zum Mittelalter und der Renaissance, in denen Marmor und Bronze das vorherrschende Material für Skulpturen war, her. Im 20. Jahrhundert wird diese Tradition gebrochen und Holz kann sich als Werkstoff gegenüber der Bronze behaupten. Klinge erweitert seine Begrifflichkeit des Holzes, indem er eine Verbindung zum Baum herstellt: „Das Holz erzählt viele Geschichten, das Wachsen des Baumes über einen langen Zeitraum. Sein Holz, das ich benutze, zeigt die Zeit des Lebens des Baumes und mein Werk in diesem Holz." Durch die Transformation des Holzmodells in Bronze gibt der Künstler dem Baum eine Lebensdauer, die seine organische Substanz nicht hätte. Diese Vorgehensweise ist vergleichbar mit der Entstehung von Fossilien, in denen sich die Kräfte der Natur und die Zeit abbilden.

*„**Nellie Angel**" ist nur ein wichtiges Werk im Jahre 1999. Wie bereits erwähnt ist dies die erste Annäherung an die Ganzkörperskulptur. „**Großer Trefree**" ist eine von sieben Figuren, die 1999 und 2000 entstehen. In Wirklichkeit geht der Entwurf für diese Komposition auf eine der Kleinplasti-*

Nellie Angel
Bronze, 1999, 0/6
h. 30 inches
Höhe 76 cm

composition was initially realized in 1998 as one of the artist's small bronzes. At this scale, a draft in miniature, the artist lost his fear of fashioning the full figure. This fright might be a perplexing or foreign notion to most, after all the dialogue of history abounds with figurative imagery. Ironically, it is Klinge's acute awareness of this very lineage and its most profound exponents that gave pause to his decision to engage with it. At the end of the second millennium, was the human form valid and, if so, what contribution could he propose? The period since the 1987 **Head of Holofernes** (and the precedents of his oeuvre then established) was one of discernment as well the gestation of style. Certainly, the frontality of **Grosser Trefree** and its grounded, seated posture must be seen in light of **The Scream** and **Solafam**. Further, it is heir to his achievements surrounding the figurative bust. However, it is arguably Klinge's most successful effort to date to convey great physical presence bound by the quiet of inner emotions and churning intellect.

In light of the breakthrough achievements associated with **Grosser Trefree**, several significant sculptures immediately follow. **Bachelie**, 2000, is the artist's first over life-size figure. Named for the stream that runs near his home and studio at Weidelbach, it was made in consideration for placement in an open area in his wife Christina's garden. According to Klinge, the outdoor context mandated the increase in size. Although certain formal principles are familiar, the grander scale encourages more forceful gestures. Currents of energy centralized in the torso slowly, but in-

*ken des Künstlers zurück, die er bereits 1998 fertig gestellt hatte. Bei dieser Größe, einem Miniaturmodell, überwindet der Künstler seine Bedenken, eine Ganzkörperfigur zu schaffen. Diese Bedenken mögen für viele unverständlich und fremd erscheinen, da es in der Geschichte der Kunst doch eine Vielzahl von Beispielen figurativer Plastik gibt. Aber gerade dieses Wissen um Herkunft und Entstehung der vielen Exponate lässt ihn zögern, sich mit dieser Problematik auseinanderzusetzen. Ist die künstlerische Gestaltung der menschlichen Figur am Ende des zweiten Jahrtausends immer noch von Bedeutung? Welchen Beitrag kann Klinge dazu leisten? Der Zeitraum seit 1987, als der **„Kopf des Holofernes“** entsteht, der richtungweisend für sein weiteres Oeuvre ist, ist eine Periode der kritischen Wahrnehmung und der stilistischen Weiterentwicklung.*

*Gewiss muss die Frontalität von **„Großer Trefree“** und seine mit dem Boden scheinbar verbundene, sitzende Haltung im Zusammenhang mit **„Der Schrei“** und **„Solafam“** gesehen werden. Aber wichtiger ist die Erkenntnis, dass diese Plastik als eine Weiterentwicklung der räumlichen Wirkung der figurativen Büste zu sehen ist. Seine größte künstlerische Leistung besteht jedoch darin, die Spannung zwischen großer physischer Präsenz und innerer Kraft zum Ausdruck zu bringen.*

*In Folge der Entwicklung, die mit **„Großer Trefree“** gelingt, entstehen unmittelbar danach weitere bedeutende Skulpturen. **„Bachelie“**, 2000, ist die erste überlebensgroße Figur des Künstlers. Benannt nach dem kleinen Bach, der in der Nähe seines Hauses und Ateliers in Weidelbach fließt, wurde dieses Werk geschaffen, um es im Freien, im Garten seiner Frau Christi-*

tentionally, dissipate through the figure's limbs. As a result, the surrounding environment is enlivened as the earth gains from flowing water. In the following year, Klinge produces **Nighthart: Melancholia**. Captivated by his interior life, the subject is a clear rumination on the introspective figure in Dürer's celebrated print, as well as the pensive icons put forward by Rodin, and, by extension, earlier masters. Stylistically cohesive with the last two works discussed, these

sculptures appear to draw great strength from the ground. As if rooted in the soil, they call to mind the trees from which they were initially fashioned. For Klinge, tradition, symbolism and form combine to suggest expressions of great physical and psychological power.

By this juncture in his career, Dietrich Klinge's sculpture is regularly featured in highly respected galleries

na, aufzustellen. Nach Klinge erfordert die Aufstellung im Freien eine Vergrößerung der Form. Obwohl eine Reihe von Gestaltungsmerkmalen vertraut sind, ermutigt der größere Maßstab den Künstler zu kraftvolleren Gesten. Die Energie aus dem Inneren des Torsos fließt durch die Gliedmaße der Figur nach außen. Die Kraft der Plastik überträgt sich auf die Umgebung, ähnlich wie das fließende Wasser, das die Erde belebt und befruchtet. Im Folgejahr schafft Klinge die Plastik ***„Nighthart: Melancholicus"****. In sich selbst versunken, stellt die Plastik eine deutliche Verbindung mit der in sich gekehrten Figur in Dürers berühmter Grafik, mit den nachdenklichen Figuren von Rodin und, um den Bogen noch weiter zu spannen, mit den frühen Meistern her. Stilistisch bildet dieses Werk eine Einheit mit den beiden zuvor besprochenen Werken. Diese Skulpturen scheinen eine große Kraft aus der Erde zu beziehen. Wie mit der*

Nighthart Melancholy
Neidhart Melancholicus
Bronze, 2001, 3/6
h. 75 3/4 inches
Höhe 190 cm

Bachclic Wd (FCiG)
Bronze, 2000, 1/6
h. 81 7/8 inches
Höhe 208 cm

◀◀

and the most prestigious international art fairs across Europe. The seated figures in particular capture the attention of private and public collectors; forms are masterfully articulated and the relationship between object and audience is meaningful.

32 **Mada II**
Bronze, 2001, 1/6
h. 84 2/3 inches
Höhe 215 cm

However, development beyond this group is a challenge and Klinge admits to his greatest hesitation of the moment, "If the figure were to stand up, then perhaps the expression would be reduced." The daring **Mada II** of 2001 is the artist's first standing figure. One precarious step forward is realized. Gaze and pose are decidedly frontal in a manner reminiscent of earlier achievements like **The Scream**. However, missing limbs underscore the degree of concentration behind such a seemingly

Erde verwurzelt, erinnern sie an die Bäume, aus denen sie entstanden sind. Klinge verbindet Tradition, Symbolik und Form, die seinen Werken den Ausdruck großer körperlicher und geistiger Kraft verleihen.

Zu diesem Zeitpunkt seines künstlerischen Schaffens zeigen bereits viele namhafte europäische Galerien und internationale Kunstmessen in Europa seine Werke. Vor allem seine sitzenden Figuren lenken die Aufmerksamkeit privater und öffentlicher Sammler auf sich. Die Figuren sind meisterhaft ausgeführt und stellen eine enge Beziehung zwischen Objekt und Betrachter her. Jedoch stellt die Weiterentwicklung, die über die oben beschriebenen Plastiken hinausgeht, eine Herausforderung dar, die durch einen Moment größten Zögerns gekennzeichnet ist. „Wenn sich die Figur aufrichten würde, wird ihre Wirkung dann geringer?" Dieser Herausforderung stellt er sich mit ***„Mada II"*** *im Jahre 2001. Sie wird die erste stehende Figur des Künstlers. Ein unsicherer Schritt ist getan. Blick und Haltung sind frontal, die an die frühere Arbeit* ***„Der Schrei"*** *erinnern. Das Fehlen der Arme unterstreicht die hohe Konzentration, die hinter der scheinbar unkomplizierten, physischen Anstrengung liegt. Wie bei dem antiken griechischen* ***Kouros*** *wird alle Energie zum Gelingen eines einzigen Schrittes gebündelt. Trotz dieser Fokussierung stellt der Künstler diese Figur, wie auch ihre Vorgänger, fest auf den Boden. Die Füße scheinen damit verwurzelt, so dass der Eindruck entstehen könnte, bereits die leicht gehobene Ferse könnte ihre Lebenskraft entscheidend schwächen. Die Oberfläche meint man haptisch erfahren zu können und unterstreicht die Bearbeitung durch den Künstler*

uncomplicated, physical effort. Like the ancient Greek **Kouros** all energy is channeled to the success of a single step. For such focus, the artist is equally intent in grounding this being to the earth like its forbearers. Feet are so firmly affixed it would seem that even an upraised heel would be detrimental to the life-force of its being. Surfaces are highly tactile underscoring both the presence of the artist and the tree, yet no reminder of the latter could be more profound than the simple plinth, replete with bark, upon which the figure stands. In **Mada II**, Klinge participates in a timeless conversation with traditions that reach from the pre-classical world through to Giacometti, and in a universal language of material directness understood by African carvers and early and mid 20th century masters alike. However, the individual timbre of the artist's voice is strong, fluent, and singular. Devoid of physical or emotional cliché, this sculpture declares a rite of passage fulfilled.

Dietrich Klinge's experimentation with the standing figure continues well into 2002. More relaxed stances and attention to organic bodily rhythms are, in part, factors under consideration. However at the end of that year, the sculptor is presented with a daunting task, the commission for a large crucifix to be hung in the interior of an early Baroque church in Würzburg, Germany. The challenge is not simply the subject as supreme icon within Christianity, but the validity of such a thematic injection into the artist's introspective and evolving aesthetic. As anticipated, a single pronounced work registers as foreign to the artist's efforts; consequently, the commissioned sculpture develops as

*und den Baum, auf den besonders der einfache Sockel mit der Rinde hinweist, auf der die Figur steht. Mit „**Mada II**" reiht sich Klinge in die zeitlose Auseinandersetzung mit Traditionen der Plastik, die von der vorklassischen Welt bis zu Giacometti reicht, und in die Sprache der direkten Vermittlung durch das Material, das von afrikanischen Schnitzern ebenso verstanden wird wie von den Meistern der Mitte des 20. Jahrhunderts, ein. Jedoch wird die Individualität der künstlerischen Darstellung sichtbar, die von Kraft, Stärke und Einzigartigkeit geprägt ist. Ohne Klischees bemühen zu wollen, kann man sagen, die Skulptur zeigt das Ende des Weges einer festgelegten Ordnung.*

Dietrich Klinges Experiment mit der stehenden Plastik reicht bis weit in das Jahr 2002. Entspanntere Körperhaltungen und organischere Körperrhythmen finden zunehmend Ausdruck in den Plastiken. Gegen Ende des Jahres sieht sich der Künstler mit einer fast entmutigenden Aufgabe konfrontiert, dem Auftrag, ein großformatiges Kreuz zu schaffen, das seinen Platz im Inneren einer frühen Barockkirche in Würzburg finden soll. Die Herausforderung liegt nicht nur im Thema, der Darstellung des höchsten Sinnbilds des Christentums selbst, sondern auch in der Umsetzung dieser Thematik in die eigene stilistische, ästhetische und inhaltliche Darstellung. Der Auftrag ein einziges, thematisch festgelegtes Werk zu schaffen, ist seiner künstlerischen Arbeitsweise fremd. Konsequent entwickelt er aus dem Einzelauftrag einen Zyklus von drei weiteren Interpretationen der Kreuzigung, mehrerer damit in Zusammenhang stehender Fragmente und einer Reihe von Graphiken zu diesem The-

34 **Crucifix for Stift Haug**
Kruzifix für Stift Haug
Würzburg
Bronze, 2003
h. 170 inches
Höhe 435 cm

a series that includes three additional crucified forms, several associated fragments, and a related group of graphics. The commission (installed in early 2005) measures over fourteen feet and features a life-size, constructed form of Christ affixed to an elongated but broad cross. Other than the Würzburg commission, **Cruci-**

ma. Das in Auftrag gegebene Kreuz wird zu Beginn des Jahres 2005 aufgestellt. Auf das über vier Meter große, langgestreckte Kreuz mit breitem Querbalken ist eine aus mehreren Teilen zusammengesetzte Christusfigur montiert. Abgesehen von seinem Würzburger Auftrag ist das ***„Kruzifix II"****, 2003, das Beeindruckendste der Reihe.*

fix II of 2003 is the most monumental in the series. Like all the related sculptures, the cross is not actual but implied and the form of the crucified deity is truncated. Head, arms, upper and lower torso are assembled to create the figure. The head and upper torso ring familiar, but the upraised arms and the extensive tree trunk that defines the lower torso are more novel.

Against the backdrop of tradition, the role of viewer before this sculpture is unusual. **Crucifix II** is exhibited on the ground at eye level, and asks the viewer to be a direct witness to the tragedy. Such involvement has sympathies with the narratives presented in the etchings of Dürer, Rembrandt, even Goya. One easily imagines an attendant role as Mary or John, centurion or thief. Should the Christian legend be distant or foreign, one cannot escape the ever present, global implications of human suffering:
arms pierce the air and head droops into unconsciousness. Anguish and death are universal and timeless. Such transcendence of plot and dogma achieves a degree of relevance that enlivens centuries old works of art with energy and meaning generation after generation. Now emotion or feeling is as much within the viewer as the object. Klinge is cautionary, remarking, "German art is always about feelings, but in the work there is always a sense of doubt." Divorced of a Christian context or details of iconography, ideals of eternity achieved may not be relevant; one is left with the bound, mortal desires captured in examples ranging from **Solafam**, to **Grosser Trefree**, or **Mada II**. Likewise, Klinge's related series of hand fragments may not register as em-

Wie bei allen Kreuzesdarstellungen ist das Kreuz nicht realistisch, sondern nur angedeutet dargestellt. Der Gekreuzigte ist aus Teilen zusammengesetzt, deren symbolische Bedeutung sich an frühen Kreuzesdarstellungen orientiert. Kopf, Arme, Ober- und Unterkörper bilden als Einzelteile den Gekreuzigten. Die Haltung des Kopfes und des Oberkörpers sind uns vertraut, aber die hochgerissenen Arme und der unbearbeitete Baumstamm, der den Unterkörper bildet, sind in dieser Art der Darstellung neu.

*Im Gegensatz zu bestehenden, traditionellen Betrachtungsweisen ist die Rolle des Betrachters vor dieser Skulptur ungewöhnlich. **„Kruzifix II"** steht auf dem Boden in Augenhöhe und macht den Betrachter zum unmittelbaren Zeugen der Tragödie. Diese Einbeziehung des Betrachters erinnert an die erzählenden Darstellungen in den Grafiken von Dürer, Rembrandt und sogar Goya. Der Betrachter wird zum Teilhaber des Geschehens, sei es in der Rolle von Maria, Johannes, eines römischen Soldaten oder eines Diebes.*
Auch wer ein distanziertes Verhältnis zur christlichen Lehre hat , oder sie gar nicht kennt, kann sich nicht der allgegenwärtigen und global empfundenen Bedeutung menschlichen Leidens entziehen. Arme durchbohren die Luft und der Kopf hängt in schlaffer Bewusstlosigkeit herunter. Leiden und Tod sind universal und zeitlos. Solche Transzendenz des Geschehens und Dogmas erreicht ein Maß an Bedeutung, das jahrhundertealte Kunstwerke mit Kraft und Energie belebt, so sind sie für weitere Generationen bedeutsam. Nun sind Emotionen und das Empfinden für das Geschehen genauso beim Betrachter wie im Objekt. Klinge merkt mit Vorbehalt an: „Deut-

Dar Croce
Book with 17 Linocuts
Buch mit 17 Linolschnitten
2003/2004
h. 17 1/4 x 12 5/8 inches
48,8 x 32,2 cm

Cruzifix II
Kruzifix II
Bronze, 2003, 1/6
h. 70 7/8 in.
Höhe 180 cm

blems of holy martyrdom. In the tradition of the many bronze heads, **Hand Number 10** and **Arm**, both of 2003, a simple, familiar element of the body comes to symbolize the sum of the figure. As parts, physical pain may not register, but the cruel irony of lost dexterity, mobility, and the sensuous joy of touch is ever present.

At the end of 2003 and continuing through all of 2004, Dietrich Klinge

*sche Kunst hat immer etwas mit Gefühlen zu tun, aber in dem Werk ist immer auch eine Spur von Zweifel." Losgelöst vom christlichen Kontext oder Details der Ikonographie, könnte es möglich sein, dass sich die Zeit überschreitende Bedeutung des Kunstwerks dem Betrachter nicht vermittelt, denn seine Auseinandersetzung mit den verinnerlichten, vergänglichen Sehnsüchten der Plastiken **„Solafam"**, **„Großer Trefree"** oder **„Mada II"** ist eine individuelle. Ebenso könnte er die im Zusammenhang mit den Kreuzen entstandenen Handfragmente nicht als Teile des heiligen Martyriums wahrnehmen. Wie bei einer Vielzahl der Bronzeköpfe sind **„Hand Nr. 10"** und **„Arm"**, beide aus dem Jahre 2003, nicht nur einfach ein Teil des Körpers, sondern stehen symbolisch für den ganzen Körper. Obwohl man an derartigen Teilen den physischen Schmerz nicht mehr wahrnehmen kann, kommt die grausame Ironie des Verlustes der Fingerfertigkeit, Mobilität und der haptischen Freude in ihnen zum Ausdruck.*

*Vom Ende des Jahres 2003 und während des ganzen folgenden Jahres schafft Klinge eine Reihe von außergewöhnlichen Plastiken. Wie bereits eingangs im Text erwähnt, ist die Chronologie eines solch dionysischen Werkes, in dem dem unmittelbar vorher geschaffenen Werk eine Weiterentwicklung folgt, beeindruckend. **„Entwurf für eine große Figur II"** und **„Entwurf für eine große Figur III"** sind zwei von fünf im Zusammenhang stehende Arbeiten. Die sich dynamisch bewegende, sehr organische Form findet kaum eine Entsprechung in Klinges bisherigem Werk. **„Bachelie"**, **„Mada II"** und die im Zusammenhang mit den Kreuzen geschaffenen Arbeiten*

realized an extraordinarily dynamic series. Although introduced at the opening of this text, the chronology of such Dionysian work on the heels of the immediately preceding imagery is startling. **Model for Big Sculpture II** and **Model for Big Sculpture III** are two of five related works. The writhing, highly organic forms have limited precedents within the whole of the artist's repertoire. **Bachelie**, **Mada II** and the crucifix-related works, are but initial investigations of a form's passage through space. Klinge himself offers great insight:
I had to ask myself what will be the next step to follow those sculptures which explore movement in space... the logical step would be an explosion (of movement), but there is no contradictory quality in that. The explosion is a movement away from the nucleus that then goes outside (away). In this phenomenon, time goes to zero.
In other words, through this innovative series Klinge acknowledges the significance of contradiction. An explosion would be to focus on gesture and movemcnt alone; this would ignore the stable and dense inner core or nucleus of the sculpture. It is the latter that has been critical to the continuum of the artist's concerns over the course of the preceding ten years. To err on the side of explosion would be to ask the artist to settle for an anecdotal moment in time rather than to approach ideas that are timeless.

The "big sculpture" series is conceptually and formally based on vegetative shapes and references seeds or bulbs bursting into life. For Klinge, such growth is more than just physical motion, but an issue where time,

sind die ersten Darstellungen der Erforschung des Weges der Figur durch den Raum. Klinge selbst gibt einen tiefen Einblick:
„Ich musste mich selbst fragen, was konnte der nächste Schritt sein, um Plastiken zu machen, die die Bewegung im Raum erforschen... Der logische Schritt wäre eine Explosion, aber darin steckt ein Widerspruch. Die Explosion ist eine Bewegung, die von innen ausgeht, die dann die Energie nach außen weggehen lässt. Im Rahmen dieses Vorgangs geht die Zeit gegen null."
Mit anderen Worte gesteht Klinge bei diesen neuen Plastiken die Bedeutung der Widersprüchlichkeit ein. Eine Explosion würde nur auf die Gesten und die Bewegung allein gerichtet sein. Dies würde die im Inneren der Figur, in ihrem Kern versammelte Kraft ignorieren. Die kritische Konzentration auf den Kern war das immer Beständige und Andauernde in den Werken des Künstlers der voraufgegangenen 10 Jahre. Unter dem Aspekt der Bewegung wäre es ein Irrtum, vom Künstler zu fordern, einen kurzen Moment in der Zeit zu verharren, da er vielmehr versucht, sich Ideen anzunähern, die zeitlos sind.

Die Reihe der „großen Plastiken" basiert konzeptionell und formal auf Formen, die der Vegetation entnommen sind und vermittelt dem Betrachter die Vorstellung von Samen und Zwiebeln, die aufplatzen, um ihr Wachstum zu entwickeln. Für Klinge ist dieses Wachsen mehr als eine physische Bewegung, sondern ein Moment, in dem ein winziger Augenblick im Ablauf der Zeiten festgehalten wird, der einen Teil der Evolution beschreibt und vielleicht sogar die Unendlichkeit. Den Augenblick des noch schwachen,

Hand no. 10
Hand Nr. 10
Bronze, 2003, 0/9
h. 11 inches
Höhe 28 cm

a specific instant captured, suggests continuing evolution and, perhaps, even infinity. These images anthropomorphize the precious, fragile moments of early plant life. Connection to the ground is critical; each seated figure has a bulbous lower torso jostling on the surface of the earth. Several have limbs that act as plant shoots seeking to join the terrain. The sinuous description of each being conveys an overall freedom in form and energy with the irregularity of anatomical detail that betrays earlier sculptural efforts. More than just a reference to organic shapes and contours of unfolding botanical life, this is undoubtedly linked to the fact that Klinge here abandons his practice of creating small models as prelude to his realization of a large-scale sculpture. Fashioning forms and compositions are now largely improvisational. This fact signals a level of assurance on behalf of the sculptor to go beyond direct carving, and to a more immediate realization of form and composition.

Model Big Sculpture III
Modell für eine Große Figur III
Bronze, 2004, 1/6
h. 85 7/8 x 78 3/4 x 123 5/8 inches
218 x 200 x 314 cm

aber dennoch kraftvollen Beginns eines Pflanzenlebens überträgt der Künstler auf die menschlichen Figuren. Die Verbindung zum Boden ist von entscheidender Bedeutung. Jede, der sitzenden Plastiken hat einen knollenförmigen Unterleib, der sich mit der Erde zu verbinden scheint. Ihre Gliedmaßen erstrecken sich gleich wachsenden Pflanzentrieben in den Raum. Die gewundene Form jeder Figur vermittelt eine überall zu spürende Freiheit der Form und der Energie, die durch die unregelmäßig angeordneten Arme und Beine in den Raum strömt, ein Phänomen, das bereits frühere Arbeiten verrieten. Für die Entwicklung neuer Formen, die sich aus der Beschäftigung mit sich entfaltendem pflanzlichen Leben ergeben, ist zweifellos die Tatsache von Bedeutung, dass Klinge hier seine Arbeitsweise, zunächst kleine Wachsmodelle herzustellen, um sie dann in großformatige Skulpturen umzusetzen, aufgibt. Die Gestaltung der Form und deren inhaltliche Umsetzung entwickeln sich nun direkt im Schaffensprozess. Diese Tatsache verdeutlicht ein großes Maß an Sicherheit beim Künstler in der Bearbeitung des Holzes und des unmittelbaren formalen und inhaltlichen Schaffens des Werkes. Am Ende findet die Kraft, die in der Plastik ist, ihren Ausdruck in der Bronze.

Es ist wichtig, einige kritische Anmerkungen zu diesen in der letzten Zeit entstandenen Plastiken zu machen. Zunächst sind dies die größten Arbeiten, die Klinge geschaffen hat. Jeder „Koloss“ wird in sitzender Haltung, die Klinge erst vor kurzem aufgegeben hatte, dargestellt. Vielleicht hängt dies mit der Auseinandersetzung mit pflanzlichem Leben zusammen, aber man muss sich die frühere Zurückhal-

Ultimately, energy rather than instability is conveyed in the final bronze.

tung des Bildhauers, die Figuren vom Boden zu lösen, in Erinnerung rufen.

Grosser Trefree,
Bronze, 2000, 4/6,
h. 56 1/2 inches
Höhe 143,5 cm

Gift of Fred and Lena Meijer

It is important to note several critical facts for this most recent series of five sculptures. Foremost, these are the largest works yet created by Klinge. Each colossus is created utilizing the seated compositions only recently abandoned. Perhaps this grounds the concept of plant life, but one must recall the sculptor's previously held reservations of separating figures from the earth. Finally, it is signifi-

Schließlich ist es bedeutend, dass Klinge in seinen größten und komplexesten Darstellungen der menschlichen Gestalt, eher eine Metapher als eine konventionelle Beschreibung menschlichen Seins sieht. ***„Entwurf für eine große Figur III“*** *ist wohl das Kernstück dieser Reihe. Die lebhafte Bewegung übertrifft die der ersten, zweiten und vierten Figuren, während sie nicht die körperliche und geistige Los-*

cant that in his largest and most complex rendering of the figure, Klinge employs a metaphor rather than a more conventional description of a human being. **Model for Big Sculpture III** is arguably the centerpiece of the series. The vivacious movement captured surpasses the liveliness of the first, second and fourth, while it does not convey the degree of physical and psychological abandon of the fifth. Freedom is at issue. Form is liberated which changes the expression of interior life. If the great blocked and immobile figure **Grosser Trefree** is a contemplative, existentialist thesis then **Model for Big Sculpture III** struggles with the meaning of independence simultaneous with growth. The challenge is certainly different, but the intensity of conflict is maintained. If earlier work inaudibly contemplates a break from physical confines in order to express bound desires, then these recent examples quietly struggle to find stability as the dynamism of life continues on. What underscores the immediacy of each situation is the physical power of the respective sculptures articulated through the conventions of mass, texture, and scale. In forms that are at once comparable and diverse, each exists before the viewer a kind of visual essay that addresses issues of silence and strength. Cautious reflection and judicious action define the course of Dietrich Klinge's development as a figurative sculptor. Understanding the development of his oeuvre over the course of two decades, between his early, tentative assemblages to the vigorous colossi of late, is as significant for what is achieved as much as for anticipating what is to come.

For Christina and Lisa

*gelöstheit der fünften Arbeit erreicht. Freiheit vermittelt sich. Die Form ist befreit, was eine Veränderung des Ausdrucks ihres inneren Lebens zur Folge hat. Wenn **„Großer Trefree“** in seiner nach innen gerichteten Kraft und Unbeweglichkeit einen gedanklich versunkenen, existentielle Fragen stellenden Ausdruck vermittelt, dann findet in **„Entwurf für eine große Figur III“** ein Kampf zwischen dem Frei-Sein-Wollen bei gleichzeitigem Wachstum statt. Die Herausforderung ist verschieden, aber die Intensität des Konflikts ist in beiden. Während frühere Arbeiten sich lautlos mit dem Ablegen körperlicher Fessel auseinandersetzen, um unterdrückte Sehnsüchte zu verwirklichen, kämpfen diese jüngsten Arbeiten schweigend darum, Stabilität zu finden, während die Dynamik des Lebens weitergeht. Was ihre unmittelbare Wirkung in jeder Situation unterstreicht, ist die körperliche Kraft der besprochenen Plastiken, die sich in der Masse, Oberfläche und Größe ausdrückt. In Formen, die zugleich vergleichbar und verschiedenartig sind, steht jede vor dem Betrachter wie eine visuelle Abhandlung, deren Inhalt die Stille und die Kraft ist. Intensives Nachdenken und bedachtes Handeln bestimmen den Weg von Dietrich Klinges Entwicklung zum figurativen Bildhauer.*

Wenn man die Entwicklung seines Werkes über einen Zeitraum von zwei Jahrzehnten, zwischen seinen frühen, sich herantastenden Versuchen bis zu den kraftvollen „Kolossen“ von heute , verstehen will, ist es bedeutsam, auf das zu verweisen, was er geschaffen hat, wie auch vorauszuahnen, was er schaffen wird.

Für Christina und Lisa

Model Big Sculpture III
Modell für eine Große Figur III
Bronze, 2004, 1/6
h. 85 7/8 x 78 3/4 x 123 5/8 inches
218 x 200 x 314 cm

Head of Holofernes
Kopf Holofernes
Bronze, 1987, 0/8
h. 7 inches
Höhe 18 cm

Head Crucifix ▶▶
Kopf Kruzifix
Bronze, 1988, 0/8
h. 6 inches
Höhe 15 cm

Autokatalyse VI
Bronze, 1992, 1/6
h. 30 3/4 x 46 7/8 x 18 1/2 inches
78 x 119 x 47cm

Head no. 55
Kopf Nr. 55
Bronze, 1992, 0/9
h. 7 1/2 inches
Höhe 19 cm

Head no. 80 ▶▶
Kopf Nr. 80
Bronze, 1993, 0/9
h. 7 inches
Höhe 18 cm

Geoparin
Bronze, 1993, 0/9
h. 26 3/4 inches
Höhe 68 cm

The Scream
Der Schrei
Bronze, 1993, 0/6
h. 61 x 22 7/8 x 30 3/8 inches
155 x 58 x 77cm

The Fall ▶▶
Der Fall
Bronze, 1993, 2/3
h. 80 inches
Höhe 240 cm

The Wheel
Das Rad
Bronze relief, 1994, unique
h. 81 7/8 x 100 inches
208 x 254 cm

49

50 **FoU (sawCH)**
Bronze, 1995, 0/6
h. 39 inches
Höhe 99 cm

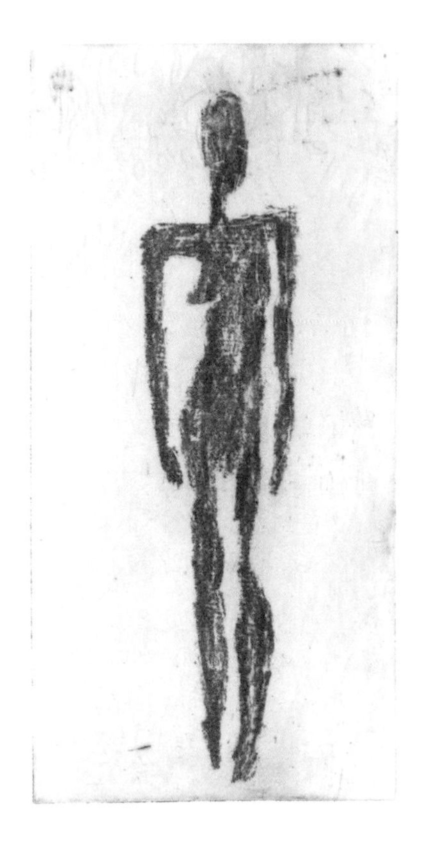

Rouge 20 - 4, Portfolio with
20 etchings, 1996, edition of 15
leaf 12, h. 10 $^{1}/_{3}$ x 4 $^{15}/_{16}$ inches
Rouge 20 - 4, *Kassette mit 20*
Radierungen, Auflage 15,
Blatt 12, 26.3 x 12.6 cm

◀◀

Rouge 20 - 4, Portfolio with
20 etchings, 1996, edition of 15
leaf 17, h. 7 $^{3}/_{4}$ x 4 $^{15}/_{16}$ inches
Rouge 20 - 4, *Kassette mit 20*
Radierungen, Auflage 15,
Blatt 17, 19.7 x 12.6 cm

52

Rouge 20 - 4, Portfolio with 20 etchings, 1996, edition of 15 leaf 11, h. 6 11/12 x 5 1/8 inches
Rouge 20 - 4, *Kassette mit 20 Radierungen, Auflage 15, Blatt 11, 17.5 x 13 cm*

Relief 20 - 04 - 11
Bronze, 1997, 1/6
h. 54 1/3 x 41 1/3 inches
140 x 100 cm

54 **ADe Prop Junk,**
Book with 19 etchings, 1997,
edition of 15, page 4 - 7,
h. 11 3/16 x 15 1/2 inches
Buch mit 19 Radierungen,
Auflage 15, Seite 4 - 7,
30 x 39.5 cm

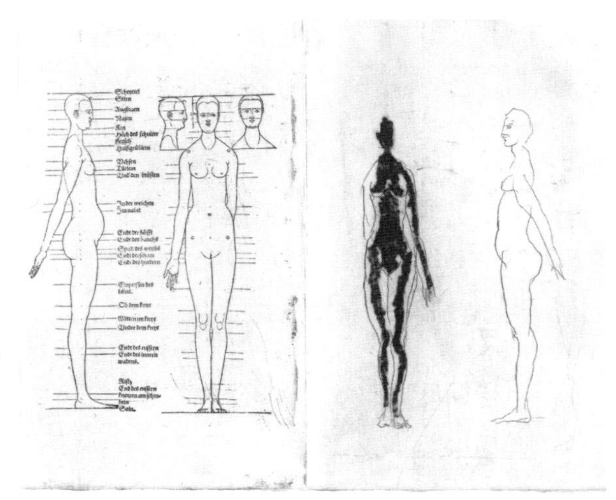

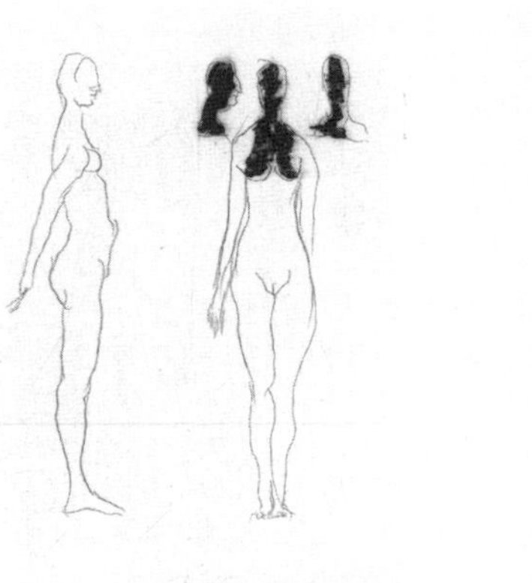

Relief E - 1
Bronze, 1997, 3/6
h. 71 7/12 x 33 1/2 inches
180 x 86 cm

Head no. 102
Kopf Nr. 102
Bronze, 1996, 0/9
h. 7 1/2 inches
Höhe 19 cm

Head no. 103 ▶▶
Kopf Nr. 103
Bronze, 1997, 0/9
h. 7 inches
Höhe 18 cm

Head no. 107
Kopf Nr. 107
Bronze, 1997, 0/9
h. 7 5/8 inches
Höhe 19,5 cm

58 **Head no. 111**
Kopf Nr. 111
Bronze, 1998, 0/9
h. 17 1/8 inches
Höhe 43,5 cm

Solafam
Bronze, 1998, 0/6
h. 68 1/2 x 29 x 30 inches
174 x 74 x 77cm

Head no. 116
Kopf Nr. 116
Bronze, 1999, 0/9
h. 15 1/3 inches
Höhe 39 cm

Head no. 135 ▶▶
Kopf Nr. 135
Bronze, 2000, 0/9
h. 10 inches
Höhe 25,5 cm

Stele Garuge
Bronze, 2000, 3/6
h. 69 3/8 inches
Höhe 176 cm

62

Nellie Angel
Bronze, 1999, 0/6
h. 30 inches
Höhe 76 cm

Nellie Angel
Bronze, 1999, 0/6
h. 30 inches
Höhe 76 cm

64 **Äponie II**
Bronze, 2000, 0/6
h. 36 5/8 inches
Höhe 93 cm

Äponie II
Bronze, 2000, 0/6
h. 36 5/8 inches
Höhe 93 cm

Bachelie Wd (FCiG)
Bronze, 2000, 1/6
h. 81 7/8 inches
Höhe 208 cm

68

Nighthart Melancholy
Neidhart Melancholicus
Bronze, 2001, 3/6
h. 75 3/4 inches
Höhe 190 cm

Nighthart Melancholy
Neidhart Melancholicus
Bronze, 2001, 3/6
h. 75 3/4 inches
Höhe 190 cm

70 **Mada II**
Bronze, 2001, 1/6
h. 84 2/3 inches
Höhe 215 cm

Mada II
Bronze, 2001, 1/6
h. 84 $^2/_3$ inches
Höhe 215 cm

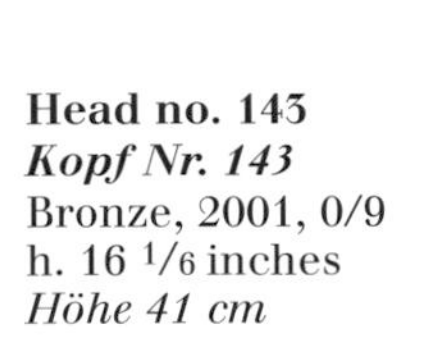

Head no. 143
Kopf Nr. 143
Bronze, 2001, 0/9
h. 16 1/6 inches
Höhe 41 cm

Head no. 146 ▶▶
Kopf Nr. 146
Bronze, 2001, 0/9
h. 15 3/4 inches
Höhe 40 cm

Head no. 165
Kopf Nr. 165
Bronze, 2002, 0/9
h. 13 3/4 inches
Höhe 35 cm

74 **ROES II**
Bronze, 1999/2003, 0/6
h. 61 13/16 inches
Höhe 158 cm

ROES II
Bronze, 1999/2003, 0/6
h. 61 13/16 inches
Höhe 158 cm

76 **The Fragment**
Das Fragment
Bronze, 2003, 1/3
h. 19 3/8 x 9 x 7 inches
79 x 23 x 18 cm

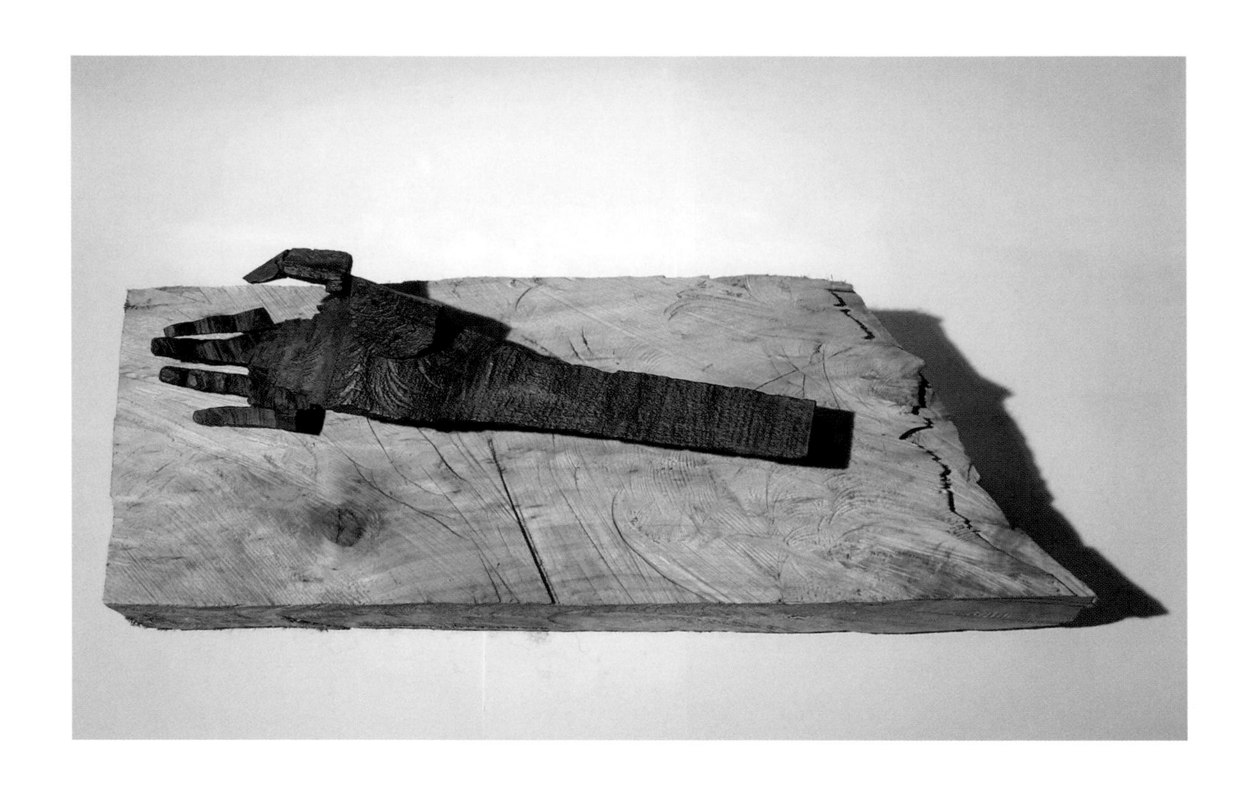

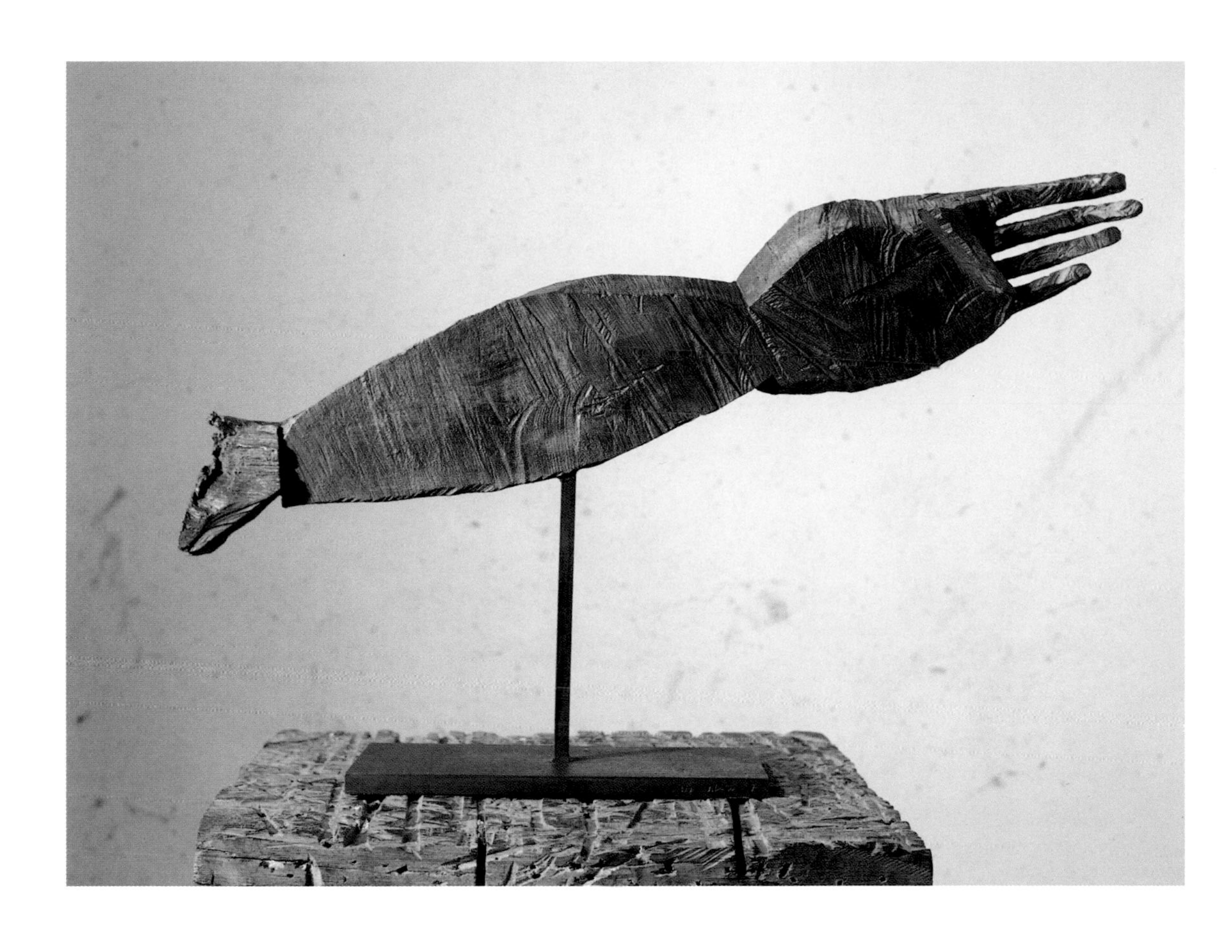

Arm
Bronze, 2003, 1/6
h. 19 3/8 x 30 3/8 x 5 1/2 inches
49 x 77 x 14cm

Hand no. 9
Hand Nr. 9
Bronze, 2003, 0/9
h. 16 3/4 inches
Höhe 42,5 cm

Hand no. 14 ▶▶
Hand Nr. 14
Bronze, 2004, 3/9
h. 14 1/6 inches
Höhe 36 cm

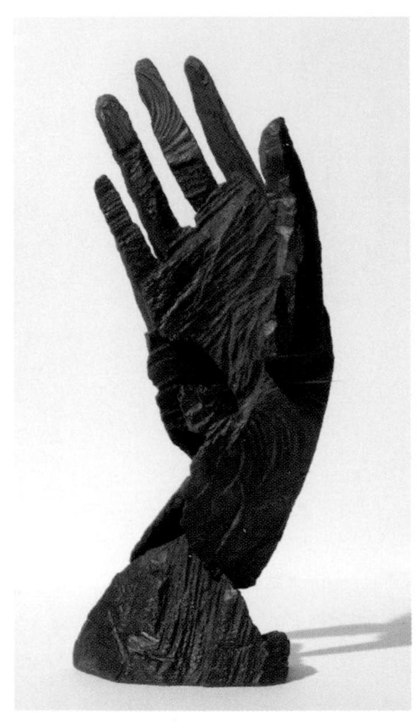

Cruzifix II
Kruzifix II
Bronze, 2003, 1/6
h. 70 7/8 inches
Höhe 180 cm

80

Model Big Sculpture I
Modell für eine Große Figur I
Bronze, 2003/2004, 1/6
h. 97 x 98 $^{7}/_{16}$ x 78 $^{3}/_{4}$ inches
246 x 250 x 200 cm

82

Model Big Sculpture II
Modell für eine Große Figur II
Bronze, 2004, 1/6
h. 98 1/2 x 104 1/3 x 84 3/8 inches
250 x 265 x 215 cm

84 **Model Big Sculpture II**
Modell für eine Große Figur II
Bronze, 2004, 1/6
h. 98 1/2 x 104 1/3 x 84 3/8 inches
250 x 265 x 215 cm

Model Big Sculpture III
Modell für eine Große Figur III
Bronze, 2004, 1/6
h. 85 7/8 x 78 3/4 x 123 5/8 inches
218 x 200 x 314 cm

88

Model Big Sculpture III
Modell für eine Große Figur III
Bronze, 2004, 1/6
h. 85 7/8 x 78 3/4 x 123 5/8 inches
218 x 200 x 314 cm

Bibliography
Bibliographie

1989
Homöostase und andere Arbeiten, Katalog zur gleichnamigen Ausstellung in Stuttgart, 1989

1990
Otto Rothfuss, in: kon-disparat, Katalog zur gleichnamigen Ausstellung in Esslingen, 1990

1991
Martin Schneider, in: Autokatalyse und andere Arbeiten, Katalog zur Ausstellung „Autokatalyse“
Skulpturen, Bücher, Blätter der Galerie Brusberg Berlin, 1992
Bernd Krimmel, in: 7. Nationale der Zeichnung Bildhauer-Zeichnung, Katalog zur gleichnamigen Ausstellung in Augsburg, 1991

1992
Martin Schneider, in: Köpfe 1986–92, Katalog 1992
Erich Thies, in: Kopf-Ansichten, Malerei und Plastik der 80er Jahre. Katalog zur gleichnamigen Ausstellung der Pfalzgalerie Kaiserslautern, 1992/93 und den Städtischen Museen Heilbronn, 1993.
Autokatalyse I-VI, Katalog zur gleichnamigen Ausstellung in Stuttgart, 1992

1993
Martin Schneider, Tobias Hauser, in: Köpfe 1989–93, Katalog 1993
Walter Jens u.a., in: Akademie 1993, Katalog zur Ausstellung der Akademie der Künste, von Mitgliedern der Abteilung Bildende Kunst und ihren Gästen, Berlin 1993/94

1994
Martin Mezger, Martin Schneider, Dieter Brusberg, Thomas Ruppel, in: Trilogie ÖK, Zyklus von 1982 bis 1985 in vier Kapiteln und acht Mappen, Brusberg Dokumente 31, Katalog zur gleichnamigen Ausstellung der Galerie Brusberg Berlin, 1994

1995
Hanne Weskott, in: Katalog „head & figures“, Galerie von Braunbehrens, München 1995
Dieter Brusberg, Martin Schneider, in Katalog: „Im Labyrinth“, Galerie Brusberg Berlin
Dieter Brunner, Martin Schneider, in: Katalog „Horse Woman“, Katalog zur gleichnamigen Ausstellung der Städtischen Museen Heilbronn, 1995

1996
Dieter Brunner, Gabriele Holthuis, Andreas Pfeiffer u.a., in: „Plätze und Platzzeichen. Der Platz – ein Thema der Kleinplastik seit Giacometti.“ Katalog zur gleichnamigen Ausstellung, Heilbronn/ Sigmaringen, 1996
Adolf Smitmans, Martin Mezger, in: Junk, Katalog zur gleichnamigen Ausstellung, Frankfurt, 1996
Martin Schneider, in: Bilder, aus Bildern, über Bilder, Stuttgart 1996.

1997
Norbert Dahlström, Eckhard Kremers, Manfred Fath, in: „Das Weinheimer Projekt“ mit Dietrich Klinge, Katalog Weinheim, 1997
Tanja Fiedler, Renate Franke, Lorenz Tomerius, in: Deutschland im Winter, Passionsbilder, Katalog zur gleichnamigen Ausstellung der Galerie Brusberg, Berlin, 1997
Martin Schneider, in: Rouge (20–4), Katalog, 1997
Barbara Stark, in: Im Fluss, Bronzeplastik heute, Katalog zur gleichnamigen Ausstellung, Konstanz 1997
H. Dilly, H. Maier, C. Ottnad, A. Smitmans, in: Druck 97, Katalog zur gleichnamigen Ausstellung, 1997

1998
G. Holthuis, G. Kerkhoff, E. Kremers, C. Lichtenstern, K. Oberländer, B. Stark, in: Werkstattbuch 1986–1998, zur Ausstellung der Galerie von Braunbehrens, München, 1998
Konrad Oberländer, in: Köpfe-Büsten, Katalog zur gleichnamigen Ausstellung, Augsburg, 1998
Friedemann Pfäfflin, Andreas Pfeiffer, Martin Schneider, in: Dietrich Klinge zu St. Kilian in Heilbronn, Katalog zur gleichnamigen Ausstellung, Heilbronn, 1998
Adolf Smitmans, in: Sammlung Walter Grosz, 100 Meisterwerke, Galerie Albstadt, 1998
Volker Probst, Die Spur des Schwebenden, in: Das Güstrower Ehrenmal, Ernst Barlach, Güstrow, 1998

1999
Gabriele Holthuis, in: Skulpturen-Museum Heilbronn, Kleinplastik – Bozzetti – Köpfe, Katalog der Städtischen Museen Heilbronn, 1999
Gabriele Kerkhoff, Martin Schneider, Barbara Stark, in: Dietrich Klinge, Skulpturen, Katalog zur gleichnamigen Ausstellung der Galerie Orangerie-Reinz, Köln, 1998
Andreas Pfeiffer, Babette Krimmel, Karlheinz Nowald u.a., in: La mano, Die Hand in der Skulptur des 20. Jahrhunderts, Katalog zu gleichnamigen Ausstellung der Städtischen Museen Heilbronn, 1999
Sechs Weggefährten, Katalog der Edition Brusberg, Berlin zur Art Basel, 1999

2000
Gabriele Kerkhoff, Gode Krämer, Franz Träger, in: Dietrich Klinge, Skulpturen, Katalog zur gleichnamigen Ausstellung der Galerie Bäumler, Regensburg, 2000
Gabriele Kerkhoff, Gode Krämer, Franz Träger, in: Dietrich Klinge, Skulpturen, Katalog zur gleichnamigen Ausstellung der Galerie Orangerie-Reinz, Köln 2000
Ines Kohl, Sabine Perzl, in: Figur 2000, Katalog zur gleichnamigen Ausstellung in Regensburg, 2000
Dieter Brunner, Barbara Stark, in Dietrich Klinge, Weidelbach 1999–2000, Katalog zur gleichnamigen Ausstellung der Galerie von Braunbehrens, München 2000
Gerhard F. Keinz in: 40 Jahre Orangerie-Reinz, Katalog zur gleichnamigen Ausstellung der Orangerie-Reinz, Köln 2000

2001
Barbara Stark, Gabriele Holthuis, Rüdiger Heinze, Martin Schneider, in: Das Gesicht als Bild der Seele.
Katalog zur gleichnamigen Ausstellung in Konstanz und Schwäbisch Gmünd, 2001
„Loplop présente ...“, Katalog der Edition Brusberg Berlin zur TEFAF Maastricht, 2001
Peter Anselm Riedl, „Fünf Grosse Figuren“, Katalog zur gleichnamigen Ausstellung in Schloss Mochental, Schwäbisch Gmünd und Freiburg, 2001
Friedmann Pfäfflin, „NvR, der erste Beatle, ein Kalauer“, 2001
Brusberg in Basel 2001, Katalog zur Edition Brusberg Berlin zur 32. Art Basel, 2001
Manfred Schneider in: Joachim Efinger und Dietrich Klinge, Mochental 2001

2002
Eckhard Kremers, Martin Schneider in: Eine Figur und 29 Köpfe, Katalog 2002
„Loplop présente ...“ Katalog der Edition Brusberg zur TEFAF Maastricht, 2002
„Brusberg in Basel“ Katalog der Edition Brusberg
Berlin zur 33. Art Basel, 2002
Martin Schneider, „Fast alles! Fast nichts!“ Katalog zur gleichnamigen Ausstellung in der Galerie von Braunbehrens, München 2002
Dieter Brusberg, Karin Selnick in: Kunst im HDI,
Hannover, 2002
Herwig Guratzsch u.a. in: Farbe, Form, Zeichnung. Sammlung Pipenbrock, Heidelberg, 2002
Joseph Antenucci Becherer in: Gardens of Art, The Sculpture Park at the Frederik Meijer Gardens, Grand Rapids, Michigan, 2002

2003
Jürgen Lenssen in: Das Diözesanmuseum, Katalog, Würzburg, 2002
Norbert Dahlström, Christa Lichtenstern, Martin Schneider in: Das Weinheimer Projekt II, Katalog, Weinheim, 2003
Friedemann Pfäfflin, "Adam und Eva", 2003
"Brusberg in Basel", Katalog der Edition Brusberg zur 34. Art Basel, 2003

2004
"Brusberg in Basel", Katalog der Edition Brusberg zur 35. Art Basel, 2004
Dieter Brunner in: Brüche und Kontinuitäten, Katalog zur gleichnamigen Ausstellung,
Galerie von Braunbehrens, München, 2004
Joseph Antenucci Becherer in:
Outside in, Sculpture for the Natural World, Katalog der Carry Secrist Gallery, Chicago, 2004

2005
Martin Schneider in: Kruzifix für Stift Haug, Stuttgart, 2005
Karin von Behr, Marion Nickig, Künstlergärten in Deutschland, Hamburg, 2005

Exhibitions
Ausstellungen

1989
Ateliergemeinschaft Wilhelmstraße 16 e.V., Stuttgart

1990
Galerie Brusberg Berlin
Galerie Fahlbusch, Mannheim (E)
Galerie im Heppächer, Esslingen (E)
Galerie Brusberg Berlin, Art Cologne, Köln
Galerie Fahlbusch, Art Hamburg

1991
Nationale der Zeichnung, Augsburg, Sonderausstellung

1992
Galerie Brusberg Berlin (E)
Galerie Brusberg Berlin, Art Basel
Galerie im Heppächer, Esslingen (E)
Sammlung Dahlström, Weinheim (E)
Pfalzgalerie Kaiserslautern

1993
Städtische Museen Heilbronn
Ateliergalerie Oberländer, Augsburg (E)
Galerie Brusberg Berlin
Galerei Brusberg Berlin, Art Basel
Schwörhaus, Esslingen
Akademie der Künste, Berlin

1994
Galerie Brusberg Berlin (E)
Galerie von Braunbehrens, Art Frankfurt
Galerie Holzwarth, Stuttgart
Galerie von Braunbehrens, Art Cologne, Köln
Städtische Galerie Albstadt (E)
Galerie von Braunbehrens, München (E)

1995
Galerie von Braunbehrens, München
Galerie von Braunbehrens, Art Frankfurt
Kunstförderverein Weinheim

Galerie im Heppächer, Esslingen (E)
Städtische Museen Heilbronn (E)

1996
Galerie Brusberg Berlin (E) m. W. L.
Städtische Museen Heilbronn
IG-Metall Galerie, Frankfurt am Main (E)
Ateliergalerie Oberländer, Augsburg
Kulturzentrum Templin (E) m. W. L.
Galerie Brusberg Berlin
Galerie von Braunbehrens, München (E)

1997
Sebastianskapelle Ulm (E)
Archäologisches Landesmuseum, Konstanz
Galerie Brusberg Berlin
Städtische Galerie Albstadt
Galerie Fahlbusch, Kunst 97 Zürich
Mannheimer Kunstverein (E)
Galerie Fahlbusch, Mannheim (E)

1998
Städtische Galerie Albstadt
Galerie Orangerie-Reinz, Köln
Kilianskirche Heilbronn (E)
Atelier-Galerie Oberländer, Augsburg (E)
Städtische Galerie Albstadt
Galerie Kerkhoff, Verl (E)
Galerie Orangerie-Reinz, Art Basel
Galerie Fahlbusch, Mannheim
Galerie von Braunbehrens, München (E)
Städtische Galerie Albstadt
Galerie Fahlbusch, Freiburg, Radolfzell
Galerie von Braunbehrens, Art Cologne (E)
Galerie Orangerie-Reinz, Art Cologne
Galerie Brusberg Berlin
Gerhard-Marcks-Haus, Bremen
Galerie Fahlbusch, Mannheim
Galerie Orangerie-Reinz, Art Cologne
Galerie Brusberg Berlin
Gerhard-Marcks-Haus, Bremen
Galerie Fahlbusch, Mannheim

1999
Galerie Orangerie-Reinz, Köln (E)
Galerie Orangerie-Reinz, Westdeutsche Kunstmesse, Köln
Städtische Museen HeilbronnGalerie Brusberg, Art Basel
Galerie Orangerie-Reinz, Art Basel
Galerie Bäumler, Regensburg
Galerie Weise, Chemnitz
Galerie Stübler, Hannover
Galerie Orangerie-Reinz, Art Cologne
Galerie Thomas, Art Cologne
Galerie Titan, Frankfurt am Main (E)
Sammlung Dahlström, Weinheim (E)

2000
Galerie von Braunbehrens, Arco Madrid
Galerie Orangerie-Reinz, Arco Madrid
Wendelinkapelle, Weil der Stadt
Galerie Bäumler, Regensburg (E)
Galerie Orangerie-Reinz, WKM Köln
Galerie Weise, Art Frankfurt
Galería Joanna Kunstmann, Mallorca
Städtische Museen Heilbronn
Galerie Orangerie-Reinz, Köln (E)
Figur 2000, Regensburg
Galerie Orangerie-Reinz, Art Basel
Galerie Brusberg Berlin
Galerie von Braunbehrens, München (E)
Städtische Galerie Albstadt
Galerie Orangerie-Reinz, Art Cologne

Galerie von Braunbehrens, Art Cologne
Galerie Orangerie-Reinz, Köln
Galerie Brusberg Berlin
Stiftung für Bildhauerei, Berlin (E)
Galería Joanna Kunstmann, Mallorca

2001
Ateliergalerie Oberländer, Augsburg (E) mit U. K.
Wessenberg Galerie, Konstanz (E) mit A.v.J.
Galerie von Braunbehrens, Arco Madrid
Galerie Titan, Frankfurt am Main (E)
Galerie Orangerie-Reinz, Kunstmesse Köln
Galerie Brusberg Berlin, TEFAF Maastricht
Galerie Schloss Mochental (E)
Galerie Weise, Art Frankfurt
Galerie Brusberg Berlin, Art Basel
Galerie Orangerie-Reinz, Art Basel
Galerie im Prediger, Schwäbisch Gmünd (E)
Museum im Prediger, Schwäbisch Gmünd (E) mit A.v.J.
Morat-Institut für Kunst und Kunstwissenschaft,
Freiburg i. Br. (E)
Galerie Orangerie-Reinz, Art Cologne (E)
Galerie Schlichtenmeier, Schloss Dätzingen, Grafenau

2002
Galerie von Braunbehrens, Arco Madrid
Galerie Brusberg Berlin, TEFAF Maastricht
Art Selection Gilg, Zürich (E)
Galería Joanna Kunstmann, Mallorca (E)
Kamp's Galerie, Keitum, Sylt (E)
Galerie Orangerie-Reinz, Kunstmarkt Köln
Galerie von Braunbehrens, Art Frankfurt
Galerie Weise, Art Frankfurt
Kunst Mammern, Schweiz mit Burkhard Held
Galerie Brusberg Berlin, Art Basel
Galerie Orangerie-Reinz, Art Basel
Galerie von Braunbehrens, München (E)
Galerie Weise, Art Bregnenz
Galerie Schloss Mochental
Galerie Bäumler, Regensburg (E)
DRK Krankenhaus Westend Berlin (E)
mit Rolf Szymanski
Galerie Orangerie Reinz, Art Cologne
Galerie von Braunbehrens, Art Cologne
Willy Brandt Haus, Berlin
Galería Joanna Kunstmann, Mallorca

2003
Galerie von Braunbehrens, Arte Fiera Bologna
Galerie Orangerie Reinz, Arco Madrid
Galerie von Braunbehrens, Arco Madrid
Galerie Orangerie Reinz, Köln (E)
mit Christina Roederer
Diözesanmuseum Würzburg
Städtische Museen Heilbronn
Galerie Schrade, Karlsruhe (E)
Stadtkirche Darmstadt (E)
Galerie Orangerie Reinz, Kunst Köln
Galerie von Braunbehrens, Art Frankfurt
Zeitgeschichtliches Forum Leipzig
Galerie Brusberg Berlin, Art Basel
Galerie Orangerie Reinz, Art Basel
Galerie Weise, Chemnitz (E)
Galerie Schrade, Schloss Mochental (E)
Galerie Orangerie Reinz, Art Cologne
Galerie von Braunbehrens, Art Cologne
Galerie Orangerie Reinz, Köln
Galerie Netuschil, Darmstadt

2004
Galerie Orangerie Reinz, Arco Madrid
Städtische Galerie Albstadt
Stadtkirche Darmstadt
Galerie Schloss Mochental, Art Karlsruhe
Donna Tribby Fine Art, West Palm Beach (E)
Klarissenkloster Pfullingen
Galerie Bäumler, Regensburg
Galerie Brusberg Berlin, Art Basel
Galerie Orangerie Reinz, Art Basel
Galerie von Braunbehrens, München (E)
Carrie Secrist Gallery, Chicago
Galerie von Braunbehrens, Art Cologne
Galerie Orangerie Reinz, Art Cologne
Galerie von Braunbehrens, Art Zürich

2005
Galerie Brusberg Berlin, Berlin (E)
Worthington Gallery, Art Show, New York
Galerie Orangerie Reinz, Arco Madrid
Galerie von Braunbehrens, Art Karlsruhe
Galerie Schloß Mochental, Art Karlsruhe (E)
Galería Joanna Kunstmann, Mallorca
Worthington Gallery, Chicago (E)
Galerie von Braunbehrens, Art Frankfurt
Andrej Gertsev Gallery, Moskau (E) mit Christina Roederer
Galerie von Braunbehrens, KIAF, Seoul
Frederik Meijer Gardens, Grand Rapids, Michigan (E)
Galerie Orangerie Reinz, Art Basel
Galerie Orangerie Reinz, Köln (E)
Galerie Orangerie Reinz, Art Cologne
Museum Küppersmühle Sammlung Grothe, Duisburg (E)

List of collections
Sammlungen

Staatsgalerie Stuttgart
Städtische Kunsthalle Mannheim
Staatliche Graphische Sammlung München
Städtische Museen Heilbronn
Städtisches Museum Albstadt
Museum im Prediger, Schwäbisch Gmünd
Regierungspräsidium Stuttgart
Regierungspräsidium Karlsruhe
Staatliches Vermögens- und Hochbauamt der Universität Ulm
Stadt Schwäbisch Gmünd
Muzeum Belden an Zee, Scheveningen, NL
Frederik Meijer Gardens and Sculpture Park, Grand Rapids, Michigan, USA
Gateway Foundation, St. Louis, Missouri, USA
Museum am Dom, Würzburg
HDI Haftpflichtverband der deutschen Industrie, Hannover
Krankenhausgesellschaft Ehingen/Donau
St. Johannis Stift Haug, Würzburg
Daimler Benz, Stuttgart
Baden Württembergische Bank, Stuttgart
Landesbank Berlin, Berlin
Mannheimer Versicherung
Gewerbepark Regensburg
The Roland Berger Strategy Consultants Collection, Deutschland
Diözese Würzburg, Stift Haug
Sammlung Südwest-Park, Nürnberg
Sammlung Andrej Gertsev, Moskau
Sammlung Peter Fisher, St. Louis, Mo/USA
Sammlung Norbert Dahlström, Frankfurt
Sammlung Grothe, Duisburg
Sammlung Piepenbrock, Berlin
Sammlung Knauthe, Berlin
Sammlung Welle, Paderborn
Sammlung Maggi, Italien
Sammlung Dickert, Capolona
Sammlung Hurrle, Durbach
Sammlung Dr. Christine Hieronymus, Regensburg
Sammlung Rahm, Zürich
Sammlung Suter, Zürich
Sammlung Galerie Peter Bäumler, Regensburg
Sammlung Dr. Priller, Nürnberg
Sammlung Tolsdorff, Bad Honnef
Sammlung Rudolph, Berlin/Hannover
Sammlung Busche/Birkner, Rahden
Sammlung Lederer, Neu-Isenburg
Sammlung Rugo, Düsseldorf
Sammlung Patt, Köln
Sammlung Osmers, Bremen
Sammlung Maurer, Boppard
Sammlung Werner und Barbara Heckl, Neusäß
Sammlung Dr. Bernhard Schaub, Landshut
Sammlung Wolfgang Reichert, Augsburg
Sammlung Manfred Jena und Dr. Uschi Nissen, München
Sammlung Werner Schneider, Senden
Sammlung Heinze, Ulm/Senden, Stadtbergen/Augsburg
Sammlung Franz Träger, Augsburg
Sammlung Wilhelm F. Walz, Stadtbergen
Sammlung H. und R. Bühler, Königsbrunn
Sammlung Gernot Günther, Augsburg
Sammlung Albrecht, Gersthofen
Sammlung Konrad und Irene Oberländer, Stadtbergen
Sammlung Christel und Uwe Herrnsdorf, Limburg
Privatsammlung, New York
Privatsammlung, Nürnberg
Privatsammlung, Genf
Privatsammlung, Paris/Genf/Beaulieu-sur-Mer
Privatsammlung, Siegburg
und verschiedene Privatsammlungen in Europa, die nicht genannt werden wollen

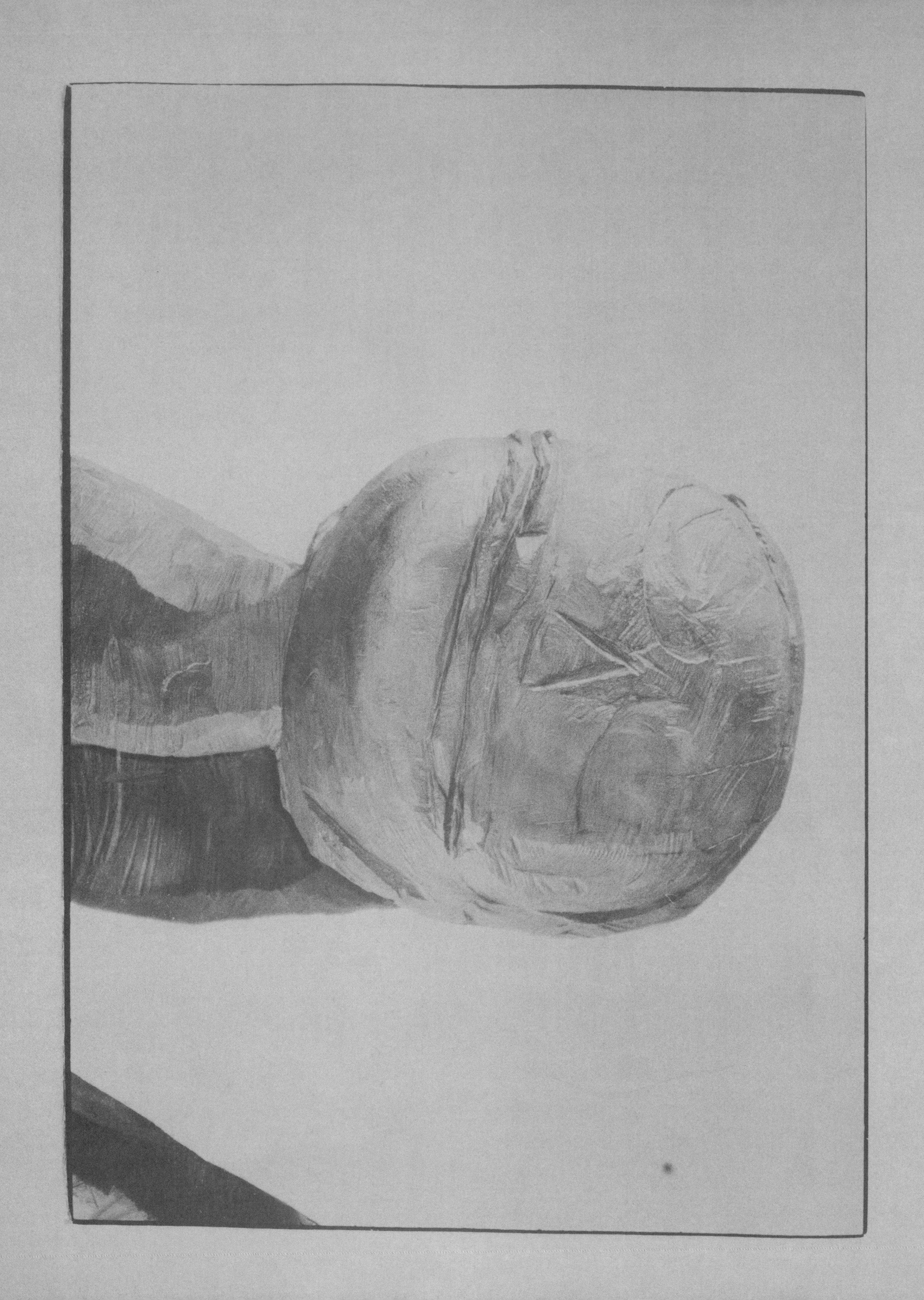